I0789770

"The Fate Of America"

"A New Beginning In The New World Order!"

By : Riley Parker Miller

₪

(The Death's Construction Book's Powering
Message From An Alliances Product From
WWIII's Antichrist!)

Written By The Writing Trinity
Declared In War From Men Of Highest Honors!

₪

"My War's Willing; Then Totaled Life!"
By – Riley Miller

The Date Of – Friday, September 25, 2015

Friday, September 25, 2015 –
"The Date When World War Three Began – And I
Knowingly Submitted My; Good Life!!!"

"There Is The <u>New World Order</u>" –

There is a secret, only one in every millions, of people, have ever heard of! Its message, is so secretive that only one of these one, in every millions, of people, can even know about; it! The demands, from its hands, are so very subtle, that only one, or one's fifth, of the fractions, of the percentages, of soldiers marching, ever goes; into itself!!

It, is the one and only, real secret! In our worlds, one and only, a few to a single few, at every institution, in each world; can even, of can in living ever heard of it; most have died! In, all of these world and all over the world, and of worldwide publications, one and only – one voice, can ever heard of it; and keep quiet, with not going – insane. Over, the marches of time, no one can keep their mouths, closed about it! It, is the reason why Presidents, get shot! It, is in the "<u>New World Order</u>!!"

"The Third World War Aged Order!" –

A Book On My Themes –

"The World War Three" –
All Of Its Other Themes Are Shown As Meant –

The New World Order
The Third Holocaust
The Doomsday Device
The War's End
Armageddon
The World At War
World War of Annihilation
The New World Order
World War Two
End of the World
The End of America
Nuclear End War
World War Three
The Last Satan
The American World War
The Son of Adam
The USA Third War
The USA WWIII President
The Sword Of Truth
The Pen Of The Heart

A Book On The <u>World War Three</u>; Who Is
Repeated After World War Two's Approaches, In A

Third Time; In A Third Set Date; And In An Third
Dimension – Me. <u>Riley Miller</u>!

The New World Order, Repeated Adolf Hitler, The
United States of America, The USA President,
Friday, September 25, 2015, <u>My Life</u>

A Production From A Whole Life; In The World Of
Three War's Willing Life And From My Time Of
World – World War Three's Totaled Book, From –
<u>My Life</u>

"My War's Willing; And Then Totaled Life"

By – Riley Parker Miller

"For the Movements of World War Three, And the American's Presidency, To Be Mine In Laws, And Mine In Business, and All Mine In Politics!"

Before Time and Place, When I Fell From Heaven; I Was A President!

This Book Is Dedicated To – <u>The New World Order</u> – To My Family and Friends – From My Side Of The Country – From God or "Jesus Christ!" Life Is To Begin– And The USA President of WW3! (<u>As Its All-Time Leader</u>)

"The penned; is named – <u>Riley Parker Miller!</u>"

The Book's Authorship of War
The Authentic Work From Riley Miller
Guarantee Of Author Authentication of Work

I, Riley Miller, have truly, and accurately, and
solely, wrote this book!

I, have agreed and confirmed, that this book's
working-minds, is from the sole works of mine, and
of myself; "Riley Miller"!

The Warnings and Caution Of The Book
To the Reader:

The caution of the message is of a word and
meaning, content. The author, for a meaning from
the book, and its message, warns of the message,
from the book. I acknowledge, to the reader, that I,
Riley Miller, am the author, and sole author, and
originator, of this book. In the book's write, and in
my authorship, or in my real name, I am the sole
author, of this book. My Authorship Is The Name –
Riley Parker Miller.

My written book, and the works, of myself. I, really
am, of admitted true and in the written authenticity
of the writer; the evidence of the book, is admitted
solely, by me, the author of this book, Riley Miller.

The author, for a meaning from the book, and its
message, warns of the message, from the book. I
acknowledge, to the reader, that I, Riley Miller, am
the author, and sole author, and originator, of the
book. In the book's write, and in solely, my named
authorship, for in my penned name, I am the sole
author, of this book. – R.P.M.

My Authorship, *Riley Parker Miller.*

All, of the book's contents, and true and false
situations, and real or imagined persons, and the
works, books, and, written works, of Riley Miller,
are all guaranteed, as the true and sole work, of
myself.

In my penmanship, as in my approved and,
guaranteed work, is by my authorship, as
guaranteed to be, from the penmanship – of myself.

The Book Warning –

This book has a cautionary message, to readers, of
words, titles, and phrases, that can be of offense. In
no place, as in terms, of the events, of this book, can
the reader, be advised.

The book, from contents, of the certain words and
phrases, and knowledge, in this book, can be
explicit, in the book. The warning is from the
reader, to be warning, from the explicit meanings,
that is in, only his language.

There is not a new world, in writings of this book.
The fictional and, true, and factual world, in writing
world, of this book, is in terms for the readers; true.

To note in the language, and in himself, from the
ideals, from certain judgments, should be used, in
the book message.

Warning of the book, is of powerful words, and
elicit content of expressed ideas, as is, to be used by
each reader. To warn of the book to the reader, is a
cautionary content caution, for the ideas and
meanings of the book!

The Book Cautionary Message –

The writer's written work, has advised caution, in a warning to the reader, from the author. The warning is for the book readers. This is to stay, aware of, this book, and its contents, while reading.

The book's message, is the content meaning, as expressed as a book, "content warning!"

Works which is what comes in meaning, and is issued meanings of the words and their expressions, is to be as forewarned! My books, to what he, is wrote from myself, Riley Miller, as from the self, or from himself, as the author. I, am the author.

To know and learn, in who is the fact-based, writing person, the author, "Riley Miller" holds history. While the reader can, the caution from who, is author warnings from himself, and only, himself; from men's names.

My caution, is in mean and implicated, knowledge – which is power. The words and intelligence, is of sides of knowledgeableness, as if in its sides; the mass of the knowledge, of man!

Depending on sides, if on sides of the book of this, from writing warning! Comes out things, from into and out the authored works. Name or namely, for and not known that these names, after worded meanings, are explicit and; of implicit names!

The book has a warning and a caution, as the
advisory notice, as of here. The author of – "My
War's Willingness And Totaled Life."
By – Riley Miller

From The Author – To The Reader
Take Reading Notice – To The Book

The notice, of the advisory, in what is in strong
topics, and the highest meanings, ever intended.
The reader, should read this book.

The warning of the topics of the book, are real and
true, from the knowledge, in the intended and from
the used, life of the author. The words, are the
author's, own used words, and is not intellect and
reasoned, to be true or false.

In reading the book, the author endorse, as in the
reader's judgment, to be advisory.

Riley Miller, is the author in the book, "My War's
Willing And Totaled Life."

The topic and plot, of what is a followed idea, and
an supporting cautionary expression approach is of
the ideas, and content, as a reader, should be –
warning advised.

The warnings, are for the explored meaning, and to the approach, is true for every reader. Due, in the topics and in the active intent, on the reader, is to address the reader. The read and known intents, from the book, is a general consent warning, for what meanings of words are intentioned to be, and the meanings of language. The content are official and explicit, from the book warning.

The title of the book, as in an introduced idea and a new kind of topic, is the knowledge and the expression, from words of the writer, is a book, as a writing attempt, as an intent of meaning, in the pages of the book. Therefore to the reader, and from a topic explained, be cautioned of the content in the book.

The book is of a warning of words. Messages and contents, of people, places, and things, is based from the ideas in the present time, person, time, and place.

The idea and knowledge are warned to the readers, as measurements of the people, places, and times. In usage of the words, names, and the locations, is in an age, and time, and in a date's place.

The book and contents, are from the mind of the author. This is a warning on the context.

The meaning usage and used paraphrased ideas, is from the impressions, of a new idea, of the world. In the words, from the content, and ideas from the reader, as in newfound ideas can be expressed.

The author impress, to the mind of the reader, a new topic. The author shows the reading audience, the intentions from the pages and the words, to be warned of write language, in age and time, of warnings, due to the main impression of the theme.

The book message is for the age, of readers. The author, in his ways, means, and topics; is that he made up all of the ideas. True to his topics, he paged the book's message, as a book wrote down, the authored and penned, of writing of himself. The written book's central message.

The author wrote down and expressed himself in, the theme, and language, and idea, his topic. He, supported the new wrote, from form, page, sentence, and language, the life of a new reader.

WW3- OWG!

Thanks, to the book's message, for the reader; I am Riley Parker Miller

The Author's Message!

The War's Messages In The American Presidency

The book's author, is new. He, had a new branded
impression, on the reader. From a Idealistic,
Book's Message!

By the knowledge used, of the author, there is a
readable warning. There is a message, and as
contented use, of important – President Ideas!

The Ideas Onto Usage, And Into Dangerous
Themes, Presidents Can Be Warned Of, Scores Of
Ways From The Futile, And Most Ways Holy – Of
My Life!

Wars, Of Over Wins, The America Author's
Thoughts. How He Wrote in the Meaning of
Words, and of the Explicit Idea.

The Warning of Themes of Wars, In Philosophy,
Wherein I Can Be Seen, In American Democratic
Implications and War's, From The American War's
Times, And To Of The Expressions Of Intentions!
The Three World Wars; In Presidents; That Are
Inside Of Us, As Americans!

As Worlds, Are Eventually Evenly Words And
Made, Not War-Based, If I Ask Of In Caution of

The Terms, In Titled Plans, Demonstrated By Fact, of the Knowledge, In the Messaged – "Holy Bible!

When Reading This Book, The Reader Must Be Of Legal Age, And In Legal Ability To Read, For The Rights, To Bear. The ability to become the one of the Presidency of the United States, can and wills, to the come, of the Americans, to the American Presidency. The United States way, is to God!

The Book's Notable Warnings Of Existentialism, Can Cause The Reader, Of What Is My Only, Concern, In What Is For The Reader, To Be Of That, What Is From Mentioning God's Church, From Christ's Messaged Ends! Prophetical "War Times!"

All Of This Book, Is Asked To Be Explained Herein, In These Great War's Book Messaged Lifeblood! Onto, History's Pages Bled Blood Over All Of The Presidential Office Of War's Deaths and Lives; Covered All Of Americans, From the Times And Living Spaces, To The USA Of America's Presidential War, Of The USA's Presidency – Three Worldwide Wars, Are On The Book Of Life!

It, Is Intelligence, And Then It, Is Up To The Third-Time, As Citizenship Of The United States of America, In World Peoples Warring Lead Role As Head Of American War Office; As A Third War's Office Of The USA President; Fighting All of the

American Leading Roles Of – "A One World Order!" A Fight For, "The One World Government!" In Fighting, In Sides for the, "American World War Three!" A War For The, "Illuminati of the Internet!" The Winning War For The – "God Of Church!" The War's Words On Wars Waged of, "If not only American, What Else Is There – In Wins Of God??!!"

A World War Three – Office Of The USA Presidency! The Ballot Votes, Are Simply What Are, Undermined By The American Public's Voting Systematic Presenting!

The Followings of the American Witness of Wars And The Missionary For Peace, Therein Is The Side Winning Of Wars, Therein Located What Is Of the Man From History's Wars, Who Dated Destruction!?
The President of the USA, In Who Excels In The America's Third World War; Is The Antichrist!

To, The Trusted Followings From Him, And Into This American Sadness And Elected History Of Wars, Measured Costliness, Counts In Morality, and Starry-Eyed Images, From The Words, Which May Cause In War's Harmed Living, The Desire Of War States To The Mind!

The Book's Demand For A War Title -

In Makings Of "World War Three's Images" From
The Costs, Of This Life Towards The Riches Of
Mine, In Intellect, And Learnings Of American
Lands, Americans In Made Out Of The General
Warnings, Of World War That Is Coming, In
Americanism In Spreading Wars – The War To End
All Wars!

To The Head of the Office of the President of
America and The World – World War Three Is
Coming! The Third World War Is Coming!

The Bewared of the End of the World –
The World War Three Is Coming – To Earth!

By: Riley Parker Miller

To The Reader's Best Interest, A War Manual, On
The Book As Is The Explained In the Explained
Topics, – Made From Myself, As If I May Ask Of
Others, To Be Of The Presidents, Until To Third
Coming of The Antichrist World Wars. Make
Notice Of, And in the USA Plan, To Obey the
President of the USA's; Choice! The Choices, In
America, Are Dying Off, As the Opportunity Costs,
Of An World Of Wealth, Enter Is the Worldly God!

In My Life, As Are in Lives from the Three
World's Wars – If, You Are Forewarned, To
Reading This Book!!!! – May, Living Life's,
Happiness Cannot Come True, Unto Yourself, In

Life!! The Losing Battles of Everyday Life, Is Never Ending, In Life's Cultured And Obsolete, Endings of the Battle, Even In Just Going, To Get A Tank, Of Gas.

Into Seeing My Themed Writing's Scenarios, I've Warned the Book's Readers, In the Intellects of the Book Topics, Inside Of What Has Everyone Of War's Wins – We, Are Following the USA's World Third Wars, And In, Returning To War, And Then Tuning In To The, "World War Three!" Riley Miller Has The Wins Over – "The President Of The USA!" The War's God's Trinity, In Himself He Is Who You Are Thinks, How He's Alive From All Omni's, Of Him; And Of The New World Order; In Good Doesn't Come; Unless Good, Of The Ages, Of Itself! The Come, Fall Life From God, The One From – Blessed As The Good And Faithful – God!

The Healing From The Truth Of The Nations, Will Come, From the Turning Around, In The Good, of God!! Even, If The Nations Of The Healing, Does Not Come? If God and His Good, Doesn't Come?! Even If, The God, The One Who Prevails Over The Good, And In The Healing, And Is There Any Good; Then We Begin Already For Battle! The Healing Of The Nations; I Declare In God's Good, Does Not Come, Then Does Come; Based In God! The Good Is Basic And Fundament, Of Healing In Our God; For Everything Under The Sun!!!

As In History Of American Wars – From The War Of America's National Free World, Politics, At A Call Of Duty, Inside From the Followings of Antichrist America's World War Three; Arrived The Messages From One Office Of America Peopled Mass Certainly Agreed, On American Wars In Sold, Ancient Aged, Times Of The New World Order!

The Decided Voting War Office From The Pen In The Hand Of One Man, The Presidents of the United States of American, President's Office! When Killings, Of What Majority Rules For Me Won Are, In To The Future Presidential Positioned Lifestyle, From the Voted American Party of Republican By The Elected Idea, To His Matters to Win Over All Of My USA War Office - In "World War Three!"

Final Home In Book Writing, Is On Books On The Laws, Of Wars, My War Office, My US Lead Role, As Everyone As All, Learned From The Powers Of My Desk!

Everything, For The New World Order, is an wartime's USA Electoral Leader, from a Presidency, for an Office, and Trials of Freedom, and Tribulations of Popular Votes, Caste as Ballots, and Consented As The of the American Leader, of Freedom, Democracy, and in Life! The laws of the land, are before time, place, and life, and can be what, bring me into power, by the will of the lands.

The able citizens from laws, high marked above, ourselves, is a New World Order, from lands, and the laws. Hand in hand, the willing powers for a freedom, should triumph, during the war, of the World War Three! In the Wisdoms of USA's President of America, Of Publicly Decided American Work, I Will, A Third World War. I Will What Are In Everyone's Americans, Must Be Cautious, To The Book's Working Parties, And Past Warring States, And, America's 'New World Order – Of The Republican Party of Texas! Lives, From True Idealism, From American Presidential, Public and Private, USA Elected Officials, Disown Their Rags, And Fully Fund The World War Three's Times!

The words, "alive," and, "dead," are truly meaningful words. Alive, in truthfulness, and honesty, in covering three world's wars, how humans exist are from meanings, of life and death. To die freely, is however we all end, and to end by decided choosing life, and for to live, is by wars. Both signals of lost or won doors, won and opened into freedoms, because making beloved the unloved, and unlivable persons in "world war three", is now the stage set, from the – "American Free World Leader!!"

America, has three duties in this life, and, in three sides of the Triangle, there are three numbers. One of its sides does what makes the past's world war, from the ages of the costs, of the worldly wars.

The two or twice-sided nickel, wins the war, in three-sixes. To all numbers, in the take-over's of sided coined meanings, the "Tripled-Six," is cometh from the – "New World Order!" The second winning's sides, of the double-edged coin, wins world wars, at the third world war's flopped side, and is into the saving of the lost souls, Heaven's Americans, are in the measured of the peace, of the immediate present, of peaces! And third or three-fold coined flipped, comes out of the shadows, the natural World War Three, and how America wins, overall of these wins over all! The collections from world war three's madmen; collected dusted jackets, from the aged, and olden books!

Americans of the all races, creeds, and religions, do winning sides, to cover all over, the entire world's identity, of the entirety of wars! One is for lost and found peoples; and another as, from winning sides, from American sacred nations. We sing songs, as forward as it, into the foundations, of my United States future's life, of what are exemplified inside the war lines. To make a golden and solid statement, the plans enter into the American soldier's plan, in the USA, single handedly winning and losing, everyone's wars, and each and all, wars!

The new world order, as the American dream, is the warning from the sidedness, from the one homestead, an, to the old nationalist guide, living homesteads. In America's soil, as is, what are merely with, "one man," or the Antichrist from American worldly lives, is going onto, whatever seas, who defeat the sailor, from wars, in the – "The American President!"

The three old-aged wars, of war times, are from America's wartimes. In foundations, where there exists, a living and breathing, action of good people – what are the costs?!

Wars, in this USA freedom's lands, are from time spent, counting the days until we are freed, as a national people. Life or the living sides, and from dead and the not the alive sides, of the American people, consistently wanted to be in dealt deals of the wars in basically, "made-to-win" – "wars!"

In the wars, of the decided American viewpoints, reason and meaningfulness come all-around. Is itself in, what are three sides in the world wars, of the sided worlds of, America's, that won the wars, over killing, and ending American, costs in the inner; lives.

The enemy always, plots. The enemy countries, from wars did cover and move all over, as a plot around the world in what, is consisting of warring places, around all, of the globe. The places of war that the nemesis hit, in warring ways of the American's innocent souls, won the global, elected' vote.

Twins, from conjoined diamonds, one for these sellable profits, and the other in the alive profits, accumulated the remained sums, of the profiting money. Wars in billions, gain to the wealthy status, from the resources in costs, and from the profits in gains, of the sellable men and women, of war.

Money comes of gaining resources, as natural man, and powerful forces of actions, priced out in theirs of interest, from Billions of Dollars in banking counted, on gross natural resources. The person of wealth, or the man in demand of gaining finances, will someday in gain of ourselves in gaining resources, for the start of three wars, from the killing off of innocent people, to the enemy soldiers, that coming home, love the lands, and its laws. They were used to dying, from its laws.

Wars are started in order to advance in goods and services, all along the road to success, and heal the blind man, into the freedom of the world. Eventual winning sides can altogether make sizing planning strategy, to gain – "War of Three Worlds." Ask anybody, if a reader of this book, if we are what, has a Doomsday device hidden and buried in the doorway's entryway, on the lands of golden streets, and branded currency; of hard-workers, and motives for accumulation of, all-possible, consists from the wealth, from the accumulated American world wars. Wars are alike in this messaged of meaningful virtues, of the lives paid at that, of what are at the expense to the owner. The "Promised Lands", of the American warring lands, are made in the plans of the – 'new world order', of the currency, of the USA's measured wealth, as in the currency of the American dollar bill.

(How the USA Is About Winning) (All Of The American's World War Three's, Truest Times, But Is In The Presidential Terms; One Presidential Office, Comes From WW3!)

Masses, of wartimes of peopled masses, ordered from the fall of man as killed, and as extinction, in the idealisms of dead persons, from all of the centrifugal knowing terrorist plots, that always aim to, scared Americans. If, their approaches mask, of the war's fighting aged lifestyle, is supposed to kill off, enemy's lands. Off of itself, of wars, from our USA friend, or allied forces of countries, waged wars and signed peace, are of penned signature at world wars! As, living life has opened up closed doors, a third America comes wise and intelligent, as the suitably put ideas, to the forms of life, inside of the word, idea, sentence, "war," and the phrased words, "world peace!" To the endings of the past earth, as "living and dying," and to the new beginnings of the new lands on earth, of the living and dying dreams; spur on the warring times. Covering of the globe, all over the world, muscular wins, are with togetherness in sided forces, as onto front languages, are from supportive people.

Approach and deeming acceptance, a new war history's walk on sandals, on both sides, of the Earth, is then flipped the nickel, as the American coin's; side in three's from coin sided tossed, from as a win, – "Three World Wars!!"

Wars, unless in caused reasoning from all deaths, in not one, but not even just one man, in sized hands can cover the "Tree of Life," and our mistakes. To uncover the hands, of time in war's funding, is to pay all of the world's war's, arming and armed forces, in anybody's mother, and her brother, the sums of millions of dollars, in costs. In dollars of spending from collected spending costs, the USA's, military warfare, costs surpluses of billions of dollars, in overhead spending. In wars then natural resources, moves in foreign lives, and can end wars by negating the valuable, dollars. But, why I am willingly accepting life, as the truest, medical doctor role played by the American President, who seeks outs wins, will cause wars!!

The whole rap of world war, from made-up times and, in the examples from this life, as in my greater life, I win, the President's position. To stand on America's soil, wind down on a hot cup of hot cocoa, and sit down by the home fire, then American as I am, I can then watch, television. Marked in, warfare and nihilism, humanity lost, not in wars of non-existing, but in lost wars, that are existing plans, with murderous enemies.

Surrender to the real living lives, from my USA in leadership role, into the Presidential terms, of the willingness, to win. World wars, came from the officers of the USA wartimes, costing as what war is to costs living money, and coming-out from what eventually is in wars, not ever came from what is not, in wartimes! The book, is written from the Antichrist's planner, leader, and marksman of the 666! The marked foreheads, are chosen for war!

Planning wars, in what is having coming plans, means all things in the world, to what it is, to have the leadership role. Standing up, into the war leadership role as followings, for all American wins; is the child. He, stands up, there in what is from a standoff, of peace and love, and killing and war! He believes in the good from other children, playing in sands, from the wars, we need to generate the national economy! To protect the USA's children, then we need wars from foreign lands. To stimulate the warring economy; winning frontlines go further, forthcoming in entering into the war ring's costs, and from the sizeable table, the cold costs from the entire wars and, then in the wartimes, allowed of that, costs of sizable money!"

In wars, and times in what are real wars; meaning occurs inside of books. This novel is, written from what is – war. The message and words, about the book, wrote down in living, and dead life, dwell within the sands, of time. The history of, the literature work, was expressed in the pages, as of old you opened, designed within parts, desired good; in deals. History's paged written exampled and open-minded opened ancient pages that are in these contextual analyses well enough are made of agendas, as sold, aged olden wars.

An 'New Time Order' sees America history, as if what are extinct thoughts of war, are opened to the paged, meant ideas, that happen after numbered and as is, as the warring manuals. Islands, as in, opened lands, exists as if are meanings, in unnecessary warring agreements, from long, long ages ago, then killing intellectually is made, in offers, then in wars ages, gone in the past. The documents of the pastimes from wars in America still are being analyzed in standard, wars from that what is, used, from foreign warring countries!!! Over, and over, again and once again, the aged "new world order," of the American one man's history pages, are documented; in this world war! In this life's, war's humankind, three wars occurring are from six kings, of the world of wars, from history as in, previous and existing, document's warred; writings!!!!

The history, as war's pages, of past fights by, the sword, of world wars of the third kind, in measures of the intellect, as in the reader, and as in his mind, do exist. Therein wars, of war and world war three, warnings. The words, and ideas, are of the readers, as portrayed by explicit age levels, warned of in, the book, in a certainness, of accurate information, or in the followed fashion, of if incidents, people, or places, are directly, as a spoken words known as, "accurate" or "true." If, there is a warning for the book, and in how the words, and meaning of the messages, can be portrayed; it is for others of reading knowledge, to the book be the readers, as if hurtful, fatalist, or, decreed, in and as the same discretion, as if being warned, by an authority, for accurate tales, and not truthfully portrayed, readerships' events. All people in all situations are not, to do with literal interpretation of every word and phrase, in this book's meaning on truthful, occasions. If, in written purposes, of the languages, this on the book, is these meanings, and these situations, that are made up, and in fiction, as false, and as true, to the individual reader.

The author from just one person's discretion is warning, persons of interest. He has intellectually made his writings, to become of warning readers, from a worded database, wherein, falsified words, and fictitious meanings, are what can differ, in circumstances. These severe warnings, leads itself, to doing wording, wherein the reader, is to be recommended to be safe, at the discretion of the author, from demoted meanings, and these values, and their safe, whenever reading books from the writer, the reader's viewing discretionarily, advised. Some adult supervisions, in young ages of children, way on up to what is of adult content, and adult consenting of ideas, are by the recommended, author of this book. By, reading these words of the knowledge of the author, in comparison of the works and the words, and the contrasting of the ideas and places, the world within, the words of genuine purpose, I think the reader will be warned, of the writing, if over too much bearing, in the life, of the situation.

Be cautious, in when reading this book, when adult's situation, from age is, a recommendation, because strength of words is a common, affect as overvalued. The expression of the words, and the wordings, of the writer's decidedness, is a warning to beware of in danger, of the thoughts and ideas. If an idea, as when expressed by a very American person, comes true, then words become meaningless.

The writer of this book recommends reading the messages from this book, as if the book was written books, to the book's messages of war, in true or false terms, of one opposite nations. The themes and the parts, of the well informed topics of third world wars, are from the expressions, in what are of reading lives from a viewer, as if this viewer discretion, came from myself, as in if, what suppositions, is in recommended, by the writer.

Permissions of the Contacting In Words of the Author –

Literal permission is to be asked, from the reader of this book, to the author of the book, as an, written letter, or email, or sent piece of lettering, of the reader's, of can be asked, of the reader, to contact the author.
If, the writer, is asked from the readers and fans, by you the readers of the book, if it is allowed, to contact the author, you may do so. Sometimes, the author in gratitude of approved voiced messages, and letters sent to his desk, then as of letters and emails, are the exchanged documents, then only used for – safety! To the author, to contemplate, read, and return, to the reader, all documents, these are approved.

Warning A Book–

If, only one, of a reader should contact the author of this book, then thus, the both parties, should approve of implicate and meaning of the book, on only the writer's terms. That is in the situation, if this is not of a book positive message, from the approval, of general consented, books, as a matter to be discussed.

This is allowed, to the reader, by the author. Thank you, for the context, that there is a world of meaning, and in a wording, paraphrase, or sentenced offending or offensive, approach to the author, from the reader, then the author, is not responsible.

The book warning, and as an approved idealism, the context from expressed in general terms from the idea warning, what is about in the words in the book, are approved, as to be safe. However in authoring the book, the author states subliminal messages, that are safe, and are not to be harmful, in what can become, very harmful, based on olden times. The writer, of this book, recommends a good frame's of mind, in reading.

(The News In Times About Winning the War From The American World Of The "USA", In The "World War Three!")

The All-American Third World War's Book!

The book I made, as a declaration of war. I won, as a signed approval form, of what I have done in life, and in how I am from America, as the willing and able, side. I, decided that as a newly made nation of Americans, to side with world leaders, to create oneness. I've, decided minded choices, and actions as by made up mindedness, of the one-sided soldiers, of war. Them and ourselves, from the presiding circle of decision, wherein the every side, is of all of only one part, is the one-sided shaped full circles shape, that wins; wars! The new forms as the shapes unfolding only, are matched with penned signatures, in world war three, of America's fates, is decided on, by me. I, am only by American terms, as the world leaders of world war three, will decide on declaration from the – "Three World Wars!"

I am, the supported election, of war. Presidential selection of follower, from warring ideas, I am safe with, as Americans. Yet, intelligent wartimes are designed by intelligent, by its world-war-Three's – Antichrist American's, war's proven minds.

The World Leaders Symbolic of One Music Man –
Whom Plays to War's Opened Wins!
The President Symbolizing American Freedom
From Choices, In The Music Of The Leadership Of
Wars, Is Played, As "Hail To The Chief!"

- The Musical Man's Choir Conductor From the
Musical Man's War Chorus!

They are the symphonic chorus leaders, behind the
beautifully written musical song playing, and vocal
singing abilities, in the notes of happy and sad,
movements and rises, that songs can be, as much as
played. A musical man, conducts the chorus, of the
symphonic sheets of musical instruments, both
human and musical, to lead the music world, with
participants of the musical world's, sadness. The
happy, man leads, all of this chorus, as his song, is
beautiful in – "As Love!" "As Love", is the
message deemed, not as in war, but as in peace, of
all over the world.

To all, the voices that have heard the sounds of
musical notes, as all being played in musical notes
and the musical letters, that formed, in the music
sheet's, hidden songs. The choral man, or
instructed musician leader of the chorus headed by
the conductor, lines of music came from the leading
from the roles, of the music stand, and as the
conductor, leads the singers, of the orchestra in how

he, waves his baton in motions, the music is playing from the melodies, of sung and performed, songs of chorus.

All of the marching bands, from the voices of unison in song, lined up for the choral deformation from choirs singing songs. Over the loudness, sings the chorus from the voices, of high pitched musical notes, symbolic of the powers, for war. Times from need, resound from singing beautifully written songs.

I, have musical, instruments. To be played, in battle of written musical songs, from all formatted lines, directed by the orchestrated "baron", as the chorus leader, plays the musical instructions, of the songs. A.k.a., or in other words, the USA's Presidents in world wars, form alliances from the winning allied sided forces, all over the surface of the worlds takeover plans to find, out! In strategies, we allow the marching of men in formats of lines to go straight in lines, marching in unison, as the wars, for humanity in lives, get much bigger.

The sounds of the marching bands, direct the formations to form lines in wars, as we are taken out as the country's, song followers of the beaten path. In USA music, the mistrust of new placed men of combat as leaders of the free world, won by covering sides by lands, in the air, and at sea. The lines from the lives, of all of the insides of the minds, and into the intellectual aspect from man, come out of the winning sides, the willing ways, in the desire, of the wars!

We, must be one of the American futuristic world wars, as formed from, dealing with sides, to the USA deeds, on the side, of warned warring wins! Anybody, in the states, from war's winning has costs of the victory, from the help of the costs of the man, of must-be situations, of humanly desire, from winning the wartimes.

War won of the life in the American circle, of winning wartime's – "US Presidents." In the USA word, action, and response, helps to happen in the standard designs of God, from the ability, from the war's office, to help riches, for people out! Those businessmen, and the industry's men, try to outdo, the output, of other countries. The America, has the public knowledge however small, it is going, to be. It is as the willing citizenship, and from the acceptable men from business. The votes polls, are open today.

To reformed laws, of the nature of man, laws are of the intellect. Wartime's intellects, are from goals of, actions. The instructed living places, are together and in the oneness, of willing sides, into war's life!

Therein lives in itself, the indwelled particles of
these instruments, to the formed lines, of the
marching bands, from what in intelligence is formed
from whose sides we are on, and in what is formed
as the past war, is won!

To conquering all the lands, and alliances of the
countries, fighting as sided by sided, marching feet,
of the war's shored island, across the view of the
mainland. In, an island lost at sea, the actions from
the war's leaders, demise the desires to the
formations of soldiers, in unison in forms of
marching lines. All in this way on islands, go out
into the world, around us, in the trials and
tribulations, of lives everything killing, into a
factuality, of judges. High at the seas, on an
Atlantic Ocean Island, stands all faced, warring
scenarios of demise, that conquer by winning. The
wars onto the deaths of invisibly warring men, at
war and in ways of killing, move to the upwards
inevitable sides, in all wins of the third world war!
Is, it heroism, or acts of, warring sides of American
victories from warring men?!!

Wins in the happiness of the thoughts of the
thinking, around the resounding musicality to
winnings from American, and Allied Forces sides,
wars are won from the instruments played and,
heard. Musical instruments, as if the musicality is
played, are sounded off! The war's march consists
of men, marching two by two, onto the battlefield of

warring sides, from every nation, every tribe, and tongue and culture. The war's wins, are from the losses, of previous, world war two, battles of the all-around warring sides, from every single fight!

The desire of beautifully written words, in the notes, from the instruments of music play of horns, brass, and the bass and the treble, play notes from the musically sounded aloud, instruments. The sound, of the flute, is like the Angels singing war songs, for the winning of the wars! We, as musical masters, won! As if, the choruses with the leaders resound as like we are in wars, we unsound the resounding, from the lion's roar, in hell-bound actions, to act alone, on the staged, <u>war actions of life!</u>

They are the, musical leaders of the Americans, as their people, as human beings, as Christians, of all over, the USA. The people, of our forefather's lands, and our laws! The musical melodies, of the continue, as to play!! The harps, and the drums, of King David, are no match, for insanity!

The contrasts of the President, and the method of ironically playing of the notes of my music, is to the highest powers, over the music! The American man, God, and His "strings and the chords," is – "The One World Order!" To, wins in what we, have played from myself! Of the world staged; music and song leader! The – "New World Order!!!!"

The battle music, of "World War Three", made notes sound, so beautifying and resoundingly, chorus and the songs from, the base to the drums, to watch the wars in; "America"!

To Live And To Then Die Out Loud Words From – "US and World Leaders!!!" The war's musical times, are arriving, in War's untied ropes, around, "The American President," for the excellence, on USA!!

To always make wars happen to the winners of American nationalism, and hiding plans, in stemmed wars in the wartime game's wins, inside of the mind attributes from knowledge, we decide as the wins. But, wins over the Devil, how do we, as Americans bring home, the wins over the Devil forces, in warring and fighting, on enemy's sides?! Always, to be in the – USA! The USA, is the golden fiddle, of Johnny, in everywhere he plays, it, to beat the Devil!!? Even in America, if in the looks, of the State Flag, in the "Six Flags Over Texas," won sides, then the Texas Flag – Wins!

Empowering and overpowering their forced positions of the world, in, "Three World Wars," therein, is the fiddler. Fiddles played the "golden songs," three times, and in the Devil's name, the boy wins! The golden warning sides, on faced

outwards, wins as its hands and body, cover in
death and, for extinguish life. He, fiddled the win!

Playing the songs of the music man's notes, won an
all-American newspaper, to write of "Johnny!"
Any man, is a fiddle player, too! The moral, to the
story, is that, all are equal, and are ready and
willing, to play a fiddle! The "musician," adjourns
the Devil's, fire red courts, from Texas lawyers, in
the Wynne family of mine. The Texan "smiling
faces", and the willingly wonderful leadership, is
even as musical roles, to every time, defeat the
Devil. The long music notes, of the golden fiddle,
is from how Johnny played, to the Devil, to win all
things, and in all defeat, the Devil. I, am the fiddle
player, Johnny, and I play my fiddle, too. And,
when the Devil, was looking for a soul to steal, I
played the American Presidential fiddle, and I won,
the "Golden Age," bid of music. I, played my tune,
to the Devil, to defeat him. Then, to join the "New
World Order." I, duly and dutifully, all over the
world, from the level, age, and office, of the Devil;
outplayed the Devil. Then, I can be – "The USA
President!!!"

Philosophy from war, into what are the positions of
plotting powerful leaders, whom lost in their
characters, what is in the golden age? To New
World Order and to winning armies, what is a
winning war?! Lead roles, that are therein denoted
as the sold and bought, golden past from wars, from

the golden aged, – "new world order," has
philosophical contentment, in saving divinity's
lives, from the grace of God. The God of the world,
for worldwide wars, arrived in Texas. The timing
makers, of the ancient past wartimes, on signaled,
times which were won, in these days, of the wars,
from one man's war dealt wars with the, body of the
– "The Tradition Of The American President!"

To manage life, is to do the daunting task of what
war, is planned or attempted, within the ideal and
copied methodologies, intellectually learned, as in
the technique from losses. We succeeded in the
new world order, in the laws of war, of then buying
the plans into this persuading of them, or from the
American publics, to change their decision on
peace, and go onto – Three World Wars!

War's frontal face I have seen, from how of what it
looks as an appearance, is in its looks, of the
worldly wars, of the fighting from American wars,
forming an appearance, from what is, appealed to
the ugly! Marks on the foreheads of children, from
the antichrist, who lost as tales are told, and as what
are from the stories told, and all of the heroic deeds,
warring ways.

"I am mad. Me, only of madness! Three wars that
won, of itself! The war is in all wars, Land is in the
envisioned allied forces, from past olden, "the
second world war", to friendly forces, sided with

America. The allied forces, that won over, all of the world war's, world stage, desired to be on planet Earth!" The lands, that are free and born American, and the alliance of other country's forces, are the sole reasons, that we are, living in the, "world war's action!" Things forming of whatever, is in another, world!

Powering, to the lost lives, of the thoughtful life, from down at the homestead, lives the Wynne family, at the tradition of the family house, in the living town, of Wills Point, Texas! Within the Wynne's family tree, the line of people, descend from southern grace at the homestead in Wills Point, in, East Texas!!! In the Texas bloodlines, we all had birthrights, in anyone of East Texas, birthed rite! Life's chosen man, is a family member, of the historical Wynne family, Texas dynasty, of the "Yet Another Glory," storybook wrote by, "Margaret Wynne Harrison." The songs of her writing, were almost as gloriously illuminated shapes, as the Sun in the daytime, and as the moon at nighttime, and as the light of the Stars, as the birthed Texas rites, as the Heaven and Earth of the stars, that shine. To the hands of time, and as relatives to the dynasty, of the Wynne family, I have won, over myself, in ways of war. War times, comes from all, its liberties, and willingness of the willpowers' laws. Lands of strong-willed laws, inherits in what is in all, I have learned, to be a true Texan!

I, have historically remembered the clan, and all of
relatives from the "State of Texas," in the
southernmost state of America's states or, nation-
states, in the status, of my family, in the State of
Texas. In family's lines, of the lands in over, the
win's wars, as live the lowest shores of the Texas
national state and freedom's shores. The lands, of
trusted and truest American laws, live an ancient
American Republic, of what or in, the state of what
formed, a freedom and liberty, Republic of Texas,
as it is called; home and freed land, land of –
"Time!!!" New World Order based laws, cover the
democracy. The State of Texas, succeeded, from
the USA, to newest founded life, as only what the
laws of the state, the rights, and the country's,
succession from the land. The open lands from
freeing the laws, and sounding the arms, of the
truest individual Texan liberties, and freedom of the
living rites, became their rights, when Texas,
succeeded. To the shores, in its alone succession of
America, the Republic of Texas landed, on the
bottomlands, of the American shore, bordering
Mexico, as its American – "Texan State."

The wars, from deaths, are alive. The news from
the stories of olden times, is made possible, by
world war three's, supporters of the world war of
America's third time.
The antichrist wins, this war! In life, antichristian
Americans die, as the dead, ends its life! Wars, of
the life roots being from the nature of man in the

antichrist, and the past history of its lands, therein are living tree roots of the family, as traditional wonders, of the olden days, invoiced in checks, and the expenses from family's finances loaned out, from fun with family love, and natural Texans. All-time knowing what is fun, for us and, only we alike, in family! Whatever, in what wars, bring if not wars, lost; but won over lives, are to the costs therein, invoiced in the checks, from the Wynne family, going bankrupt, from bills. What is now a Texan, is what from known about historical roots, therein is, a big Texan member's family line, of relatives from birthright, marriage vows, and lifelong wills, and, rituals from, family line. The shadowed tree, lies hidden family deaths, in the past wars.

From famous Texans, on arrival of parties, in how America talked of above and beyond, well over, one hundred and fifty, years ago! Wynne family, of five hundred related Texans times from aged lives, in the living clans, of the Texan, Wynne family lifestyles, and traditions of the Dallas, Texas, crowd of, family members, from Texas, in the American "USA". Family's stories, born long ago, always seek out, the same mark, on the humanity's frontal faces, to see the standards at fun and sought out lives, Wills Point, in Texas! Fates from ourselves from whenever we fight a war, life came around, giving not at alliances but, intellectual discourse, brought forth in its, sold general settlements.

The life of every tale, of the, "USA War!!!!" For the Antichrist's American, positions of power and involved roles of leadership in acts from brave ambition, converting the freedoms, of the warring sided versions, of the American souls, involved inside of the office of the President. In intelligence, we are the historical channeled winning sides, of the US movement, of – "Antichristian America!" War history's third, world war, is from where I got my vision from, in Chicago, is in what as, to endue me into an oath of office in war, that was to lead all of America, in "World War Three!!!"

This is as one man, and as in being one US President, in fighting of the third world war, as its solely accomplished, envisioned man from wars!

To fulfill the designed agendas, of the consignment of the pastimes' war deaths, in what this is happening in world war, happen as the design and equality, on the laws, for justice and of the "USA President!" Writings, on war books, made all of the USA, to warring intelligence to win! Allow people, to eradicate the forces, of darkness.

In history from living life, if three wars, is made by me, and then I make the deaths inside and out, very happening. I am a natural born, Texas citizen. I, grew up, the same, as any other, American. Yet,

my life is not yet, that of a soldier. I, have opened
up, the door, to war! I, opened the pen, with bold
letters, and red ink, to signatures of all of the
American Founding Fathers, or US Presidents,
sealed by God.

I write cursive letters, of my pen in hand, I wrote
wars. Won in my own writing source, we held all
of, writings sacred. In the ending of times, life as
the personalized life, follows any one, from any
thing, waged on the wars what is then waged, on
American, liberty. Someone from American lives,
is the truest kind of one national victorious man,
made liberating laws and lawfulness, from
legendary and pastime, lands of freeing; soils.
Hand and boned skin, not all tried and, tried and
truest, are wars, that are only wars. To this ends of
days, and in history from wars of won, times one
and only, complete the cycle of war! I written in
words, that follow from actions, made war.

I've habitually formed, new habits of the made
wars, in the times of new world order's, social and
political, office, from the war desk, seeing things,
actually from my ownerships, of the wooden desk.
I, won in my hands, the sword. The pen over the
sword's stone, taken out, of the world wars, that are
as the victory, in every hand won.

These pens, and sword, as drawn oaths and offices,
from spending times, in my lifetimes, came out of

what are from collaboration, in the new world order of the age, end of penmanship or penned writings, and ended winning of wars. Swords, and truths, pen and stone, unleashed from world war's nuclear age, of war. Riley Miller, will to have wars declared, war in the faced following, onto the worlds, of the world leader. The mindful, and intelligent, brains of the soldier, have found a new leader of American freedom, and justice. To endings of the world, we have won this surmising task, in itself as a daunting task of surmising knowledge from difficulty, proven one day, onto this day in time, to have won, all world wars. To sell souls from military soldiers, are to following parts, of wars and in this lifetime's peace, obey these instructions of war, in the new world order, of every common American. Do not discover evil souls, in the evil's; of ways, to the good of Senators, of the USA!

The three sided arguments of life, are as applicable, as what are, in a period of, 1. The USA Intelligence, 2. In World War Three, 3. The American President, 4 The Presidential Staff and 5. The Bible Antichrist, 6. The USA End Times; to wins, all from its, over everything. Lifetimes, I have tried wherein the USA public disagreed and publicized television, on the war ring's sides, and war's viewers, of me, that can become an available publication, on the, Wartime's Manual On WW3.

Inside of the book, is writings in the instructions, onto wars, and battles being fought! Wars, onto the American manual writings, on the desk, of mine at my parent's, house. Its, what is, ever the made-in and Washington D.C. man's, what is for the sole use, and sole distribution, for this American wars designed system, of the American, "World War Three." I, am the man, whom to all, is writing into these books, that are in made to succeed life, and that are inside the art of living, that is in the America's dreamt, living ways that wins, all-time's over the intelligence, of – "WW3!"

America, in the endings from everyone's life, and in the beginnings of everyone's deaths, we complete, days of our country, from wars to create, three wars – overall in its –"World War Three." I, am in the American President's Warring' Office!"

This is the battle plan, for this "New World Order." I am on the side that wins. The battles and wins, to the point, from the Americans, would be whatever, from whomever, wins my war, or my – War Office!" For everyone, to "Follow The Yellow Brick Road!"

I am, Riley Miller! And I am, war's writer. In, this book of my work, I sincerely worked times and times, again, to simplify my philosophy from wars. It, is that war is good in the USA, for something,

named all of us, as America's, followers of a Great
World War!

America as in Antichrist of war, is timed as
overtimes, in terms of a "third world war". To be in
the shores of an American – wins!

Warring philosophy, of man whose words I am in
the endings for warring times of my life. I won,
over sentenced deaths, of soldiers, by myself in
office, future from all, from the world war III, at
work.

I, am in the beginnings, won are that from slavery,
and of freedom's notorious voiced USA servants,
made of the promised land of remade winning, from
sold warring surmising, proclaimed peaces.

We as Americans, won of the beginnings, and in the
office of wartimes, a world ally and a new
worldwide humanity, will end, all of the days, of
this war.

The annihilation of humanity, from what is called
the American third democracy's war! The
American Americanism automatic aged weapons,
are from wars, are over deeds, of humanity's sold,
battle-born, and American armed, countryside,
worldwide killing machines. towards entirety of
the armies sizes, seize an American battled state, or
Warring Superpower!

The proliferation, of one man, "World War!"

The war is on, and in this book, of declarations. The war's independent and fighting book's sold message is to recruit all Americans to world war, of America's three, or, the American third time. Instructions in war, of literature and powers! This is on the manual, onto these powers, of the insane book, in intelligence. Now soldiers, are for war, become recruited, programmed minded wars, from the fighting worlds, of America. The third America, won over every Americanism's started fighting, from the wars, and soldiers, from the fighting, of the ancient times, of the America independence, to win again, in our nation's, "New World Order!!"

Only America, wins three wars. A new ordered oneness, of a new professed birth and admittance, came in the United States of America, President's office. The President Barack Hussein Obama, is the name, from the America's, leader. In ages of war, and in moldings the form from freedom, the lands of America, participants from the model age, is another third, world war's age. To winning wars overnight, the careful planning of powerful sources, firstly knows America, and secondly; recruits worldwide USA, wartime's winning, dominating sides. The third aged, warring America, is of the American – "Third World War!?" The fighting of

soldiers, the recruiting of soldiers fighting, then the
soldiers of America killing, the US is fortuned, for
peace!

"The USA!!!" The President of the United States of
America, is the leader of the "free-world!"
The War Office, in is warring ordered plans of war,
sides within the homeland, the other worlds, and the
third age of the man – in New Order of the World.

I willed, to formed proclamations of justice, and
decrees for freedoms, in wins over all, of every
land, culture, and nationality.

Land firstly established as, "America's War!" The
highest position of power, in the nation of,
"America," is the President of the USA! Inside of
war, in the intelligent life, of the foreign lands, and
tested famed countries, and not lands on this
surmising positioned countries, the best from the
lands, is the free-world, of the USA, in figures of
powerful people, and leaders, and positions of
Presidents from other nations, we can, "Win USA's
War!"

From our times, and the circumstances, from
everyday livings, and unto another everyday dying,
units of uniting, all of America, as leader of the
third world war. Laws, measure and, spoken in
word and in writing, a deed beyond, themed storied,
world-war three, of the soldiers! Always, in deeds

and works, the President of the United States, is elected in the public office, for popular vote! For the most impressive book, on war of themed office, concluded three worldwide wars ago, and announcing to bring – "World War Three!"

In the Office of the Chief of Staff, or the Presidential duty, attention to the plus and minus, of war, is of sides! Americans, always picked as only Americans, die to live, the greater life, that I hope concatenates the manual for war, in the hands of good personalities can defeat the evilest personality of, arguments of wars.

The third war, is mine before the Doomsday war, begins and ends, in "Nuclear War!" Americans, warring the battles, and choosing the world war, shall see a winning world, over what is evil, bind and ensnare, nationalism and democracy, over laws of our country! The Oval Office, the White House in D.C., and the Senate, House of Representatives, and the Staff of the American Presidency, is all summed up, to wars, even American, sided wins, defeating deaths the USA, way from life.

Strong willed, reading books, the High Seat of American roundtable, the hand and chair, is willing for the Christian leader, in choices to sit in the seat, in highest precedence of the one man's nation. The followers in parties, from American's national states, the USA, by one choice of one voice in

actionable chairs, from Senators, supported side of laws, by matters of deskwork, in conjunction of passing of the bills, in wooden support, the President's chair, pen, in hand, and the desk, opens, and closes, the door, the hand opens!
Welcome home, Riley Miller, we should enjoin to the fourth of July, American beauty of lands, flags, and stripes, of red, white, and blue, on the American flag.

To be in times, of World War Three!

Duty, Service, And Honor of the Third World War Times – Dedicated in Full Life, Into Biggest Star, Homeland, Free-World – From Texas, To Entering Countries –

To Enter Into The Winning Sides of Freedom of State of Texas Republic, Texas Tradition, Texas Great and Big and Lone Star State's, Honored Soldiers, The Tried and Truest Birthplace of Mister Riley Miller –

The Texas Birthed Stars, In The Wynne Family of Texas!
The Fame of Members, Miller Family, of Riley Miller's Fortune's Roles of All Trusted, And Official Families!

To – The Great State of Texas!
To – The "United States of America"

To – The United States of America's Presidential Roles, and the Representatives of the Oval Office From the USA Presidential Position, and the USA majority elected voting count, the President race for Office, from the Minority vote, the USA's Staff from workers in the White House, the USA Senate and its Represented Members of the US Senator Floor, the House of Representatives, and to Congress!

Inside of the mind, of my Wynne family!

The United States Presidential Oval Office, and to the USA Senate, of the House of Representatives, as my native Texan, lead role as life, wins as the Great State of Texas – "Wins WWIII!" From my minor role of writings, for wartimes' President, and above anyone elected, I have won it's all, and I've won, everyone in all three times, of the American war's, titled books!!!

I ask no to, other writer, as theirs in wars, of these comparing myself, to Prince William (Wales), from the people from who know my books! To the Electoral College, of the Popular Votes, for the – "USA Presidential Title!"

I, have won, the world's over all the forces, in this life, and so on, in the – "Life As Wins!" Or, the Wynne's family, from Texas.

Alliance, of an impossible job, does to makeup, an official leader's role, in the third world war, of world war three's, persona, in the Trinity's, from Texas! A war story willingly told, of persons, in office representatives, World War of a third time, in Doomsday, Texan, in starry eyes! I wrote over ninety books, as in, written in an imagination book's world, of the United States people, of the American states. I cannot attest, ever being, for myself, I live in living, as Christ. As, good as gold, can I sit, and write in the best-ever, ninety books, of the mind's end, as happens the power at the end's promoter; as another literature writer's life, from a lifelong role of mine, in what I wrote, how as, a numbered list, of – "91 intelligent books!"

USA's Presidential life, in all the life's Bibles, as from an aged Kingdom secretly, indelibly planned, and hand written, as the books, on the dull life, of mine – "For An American President's Desk And War Office."

As By The Author – Riley Miller, As The Writer!! (For The Reader)

As American, Right and True, Natural Texan – As An Christian And American New World Order's;

Own and Loaned; "USA Presidency" – The Life
From World of, "World War Three"!

Wartimes –

My Living Strong-Willed Persons, All Win War's
Together, In Their Life's Games, Found Out
Everyone In Our Lives' Business Deals; From
Therein Politics Of Circles, At The Top's Wins
Above Christ, Won On Popularity Votes!

All-Knowing God's Willing Texan State
Republican, Christian of Churched Of The PCUSA,
I Love Game of War's Books!!!" With – The
NWO!

My Goal to Win – "The New York Times", Best-
Seller's Lists!!! The – WWIII!

"My War's Willing Then Totaled Life"
By – President Riley Miller

One Quote As In
For World War Three –
(The Second Adam)

The rebirth, of Adam, as my depicted soul!!! The
advent of world war three, is the fall of man, and
the reinvention of, the human man. His desire,
seems to be, to have the fallen knowledge, of man.
Adam, fell in the beginning, then this will also,
happen once again. "

Chapter 1 –

All War Is Inevitable –

As of now, in America, there are winners and losers. The entire country, is of leaders who, run the world from itself, sited is in these times of need. In the Holocaust, of WW2, came Hitler.

From Russia, the "Cold War!" And the US, terrorists??? I, will not ever, forget – "9-11!" The whole world, watches. America is its friend. But, what happens in Antichrist life when, all nations are from – "War Evil?"

Will, all Americans, still live, their life, to the fullest? I, do not know, ask "Young Life!" Ask, "Joe White!" Ask, "Jesus Christ; Our Lord!"

In, the year of 2000, I saw Heaven. I saw castles. It is in a vision.

In, 2009, I saw the – "Antichrist." He, ruled with an iron fist, that is a – "666." He marked everyone. He was the mark. He, led us all, into World War Three! I, was in, vision. Now, I have an, "attitude." I think, I can lead, the American wars, if I am the hero of the story.

However American wars win, and from the costs of war, Germany loses, the last battle. The Americans,

in the costs, of the fairy tales, of stories, in the
everyday life of mine, came from data. The data,
from the computer, keeps records, of USA
knowledge. The Illuminati, we all see, just watches,
all of, the Antichrist – "USA!" In world war three,
I am the victor. The whole world, watches me!

One day, I've seen all this data. All I did is, "look".
Then, what appears in USA data now is, however
the, "New World Order," became mine, of the
Illuminati, from America. I, now will, fight for you,
and I will win! The America I knew is willingly
mine! I, shall win, everyone overheard glory. One
day, I want to win. All of the world, I will, this
want, into winning. This is to belong, to my, world
will. I will join, the Internet's Illuminati.

From this data, the illuminati, controls the world.
The entire world version, of World War, is of
World War Three. History's story is the America's,
"black magic". This enemy, I must remember. It,
Wars, itself.

The USA's Illuminati, and in losses, I, do not know
how, that World War Three, will ever, end up as
American.

I do! I know how! This is it! The world war three;
it will begin now. Show this battle, which is an
everyday battle, which it is, up to us, as. To stop,

the American tradition, from losing, ends this confliction, of the American flag.

We all, in victories, must win. This war time, just has to be, over wins. This country stands the test of time. Eventually, our USA will win, over all.

This stands up, and into alive in the new aged, "USA People!" All, I know in this new world order's time, is that we will win in, the world war of – "WW3"!

Supporters, from the streets, of Babylon! All nations, win the test of times! America is, to solve all. Heaven, and Hell, knows. The world, and that of which tells, the story's entire plot! America, wins! If, of World War Three, then all will, win!!! I promised, all of you, only to this, factor – "to win!"

Words Of Wisdom

"To cause having life, to be from what America decides, there must be a war, and in its place, arrived in this place, the sides of good and evil, to overcome the injustices. Only, one winner!"

– As An American Fallen Soldier, I Fall Off The
Planet's Edge – In to the, "New World Order!" The
Return, To Earth, From Every Fallen Race.

- Riley Miller

From the American side, of this story is about, only
wars. In the "Nazi Germany days", wars won.
Histories, decide! Germany, knew this is about,
how the American war, loses. That negatives, is if,
all madmen, control the world. This is, from the
new world order, and from America's losses. This
country, wins with the New World Order. There,
are peaceful states, of the order. The world order's
callings, is to collect the collect call. Presidents,
own it. Delegates, decide on it. And, America
reacts solely, to itself, in laws.

Losses of the life from our country, all tell about the
victory, from the lost lives that are, in the daily,
battles, and wars. A war, of World War Three, is
inevitable, in the history, from Americans. Only the
good side wins.

The warring countries, in this time, are China,
Germany, and Russia. The wars, at the endings of
the days, are the Antichristian, Anti-American wars.
They are counted, as God's Holy Bible, of
meanings, that we cannot fathom, with wars.

They are the top dog's, biscuit, and bones. They, as
Americans, are the top dog's, law abiding
citizenship, and respected councils, from whom,
lose the war. Never-ending stories, plagiarized, the
Holocaust, as what the World War Two's, endings,
condoned. This is, the moral of the story, which as
of one Christian, in the world, I, have made
significant, progress, in this life, and, in Heaven.
Why Heaven, is only an idea?

In my life, I cannot fathom how life, on the Earth, is
history's lie. Even Germany's, feared Adolf Hitler
won, WWII! An autocracy so big, that from the
Holocaust museum, the victims were wiped clean.
The entire beautifully worked, tale of soldiers! An,
entire country, became blamed, of victimized races.
The Jewish, people were, so lost.

All, demands of his philosophy! All due to fallen
times, what is historic, is due to the fallen
knowledge, from the snake. Why is it in life that
won over Jesus Christ and God and the Holy Spirit,
why evil wins? Why, is it to everyone, in this war's
pastimes, of death's life, and of this, world war
three ship, comes the sinking sailors? The man of
history's life, that fame, power, and glory, cannot
forget – 'World War Three!"

Some say Communist people, are victims, of World
War Three??? Therein life peaces, is not eventually
traced back, to America, as one country!

There, are also China, Russia, and Japan. The countries, of sin, are these countries. The Nazi Communists lost of World War Two. Their plan, from the Communists, is to make the whole, "new world order", only the enemy, as the country, of theirs to lose. The book looks good in ideologies, but the enemy's contextual analysis, is eventual.

The found life, from the underground, of America, eventually shows, its face, in WW3!! The version of life, for the poor, is starvation. The mad world, war undoes in America. The innocent, of counted lives, are hidden from countries. These treasures in Heaven are only, from an afterlife. Love of thy brother, lies from the heart to hell, spoken in tongues, hiding, what cancer is hidden in courts, of justice. The nicest world, of everyday life, is all gone. Just picture hands of history, made in liberty; on this title of war, from justice, in the US "Supreme Courts!"

Whoever is evil is dead? Whatever is in lying goes to jail, on Bibles? What costs of life? Whose surrendered life is made out of American history's freedom? Who is controlled by a false desire? Why, is to make God proud, in those whom loved, an evil life? Why is the best, of the best only, if surrendered?

Why is not, one man, always not to a false religion?
We are definitive to the USA's fallen soldier, as to
everyone.

If in worldly evil times, we win. In world war
three, or Texas in true world wars! Why, is all
those victims, came from, knowledge? Those
whose image we reflect, as our fallen idols, realize
war, as evil. Why is the fallen man of Adam, from
the history of doubt?

Do, you really know me, or my evil in the thoughts?
I know your living days, on then thinking lives, of
your own, eventual thinking! I am not, why you
are, the thinking man, of thoughts!

I have a good country. I have forgivingly, thanks
Adolf Hitler, for World War Two. I must
respectfully, wanted to bring this world, into the
peace of the world. Go towards, the goal. Make
my mark, and stand up, to be a, true hero of, "A
Man America's tradition".

God came into the world. He desired to be, loved
as every good American, are to be loved! So much
happens in war, from that in one land, and in
another lands, we still are fighting, clashing in
sides, gone mad in wars. Freedom, is freeing, in the
lands of war. History is one big, lie. In this history,
there are world wars. In the life of mine, I believed
in God.

In war times, we are all alive. We have democracy
in life, and in this, living democracy. The life, of
mine is freedom based. Intellect in power, control
end and beginning, as freedom based, puppets.
Puppets; are not the masters. That is solely, it, in
wars.

Puppets are ours. People, will win wars. So will
puppet masters, if they believe in us. Why believe
in power? After three wars, we are exampled to
win. Americans, to the raw power, directs why
democracy, only wins, in world war three.

Sands of new times are covered, over the sands of
ancient America, in the ancient aged old times. We
all, arrived on earth, from an age old order, of the
age of sold, histories.

Now, after old times, we've recovered. The new
age ordered, of the man from the war. We, at these
times, are already, at an age, of war. Following the
ancient Freemasons, is the 'new world order," of
man's, lost democracy. War, in the golden times,
when democracy ruled the country, was in the
Founding Father's story, of America.

Stories are told, from history's pages. To
American's wins, which are from what history's
wisdom affects, see in the eyes, of an old man. His
worldly perspective, completes days, of wins from

war? By the graces of one man and war, I thank, ancient times that were hard. All people have lived, in the ancient ages, on the display, at the history museums.

Forget, that in needy times, we are to be liked, in their religious persecutions. All, by the British Americans, on the war's terms. The absolute wartimes, count down to doomsday, when Armageddon, happens, to innocent people. Why in wars, are wins only? To be just in fight, that is in fought, to win? In this, is our America? The battles of Armageddon are not fought, to be won!!

The history is the best, at war! I still, have lived life, in its studied, nature! I sometimes, really cannot judge; of Jesus Christ, in whom, or is in God. The American soil grounds, is into the chosen lands, as if we go, ask until I am going, onto war. Lands and seas, as if, we are counted in America's number, are in the wars, as is of lost or won victories. Our history, on open pages, is made of lands to winning sides, and seas, to winning countries. All will, win. We will win wars. The war's property, on winning sides, is from winning or losing sides, of the world over.

The history that we are in, is then land chosen. The playthings that we grow up with are gone, unless we win, over American's soul, in its entire all. The choices, in all countries, are on, whomever, are

dependent on whom, have the winning sides. We,
all love war. The land of the free, is not dead, but
alive.

Due to wars, we are lost, in living. Three sides, to
all winning, of three wars, are our, mark. I, want to
make, a mark on man.

One person's, new world order!!!   But, his is, the
principle of this all, therein is into, the safety, of the
country's life. If one country attacks, on America
soul, as the fired shots, fights back, then in war's
life, from these losing, situations, comes losses,
from the President of the United States of America.
But, if a President retaliates, he dies, themselves as
countries die, and all hell willing, he breaks loose,
over history's, all. The President, can be shot. This
is the worst crime, in thinking's nature.

We always, must account, for all lost lives. The
world's blamed, die off. The numbers, from times
at hand, of individuals fighting in wars, came from
wartimes, then come from history, as its pages
unfold, from world wars. But, we are never the
puppet-masters of democracy, or the puppets from
abuse of justice. We are all soldiers. We, win wars.

In books, and inside writings, we exist as but just
soldiers, of fortune. By, having lives, lost, soldiers
lose, what are in lands needed, in times of war. The
absolute winning side is America. I have sold this

idea, to many people. The history is, from that which is being, on all the sides, of their justices, and is in lost countries, and the lost democracies, of America.

How we live, is in how we are to swim to the shores, together. As one, of the greatest American body of water, the Biblical Jesus Christ, walked on. Win its pride, and then I can make, these men, to the shores of history's America.

To win, in just a price, to pay, there is no cost of amounting, in deaths. Towards the day, when we win, three world wars, the hand of the ancient Serpent, or "Dragon", is covered. The United States of America's, best followers, are the United States of America's followers, and are in, the newly made loved life, of this life's living. Living creeds, which is to not ever help all people, is to help you, to all my riches.

My life is centered on Young Life camp's people. I row, in easy times. But, we are in hard times. Wars, are in this country. Deaths, in tomorrow's times, are to belated, irony.

When wars happen, the war's camera will film. The media, from the times of world war three, is how we will communicate. We, came alive past doubts, arrive of the countries of war.

So is talk, of the New Jerusalem. I, find out what this is, with Jesus Christ.

I am paddling harder. I am, knowingly, am increasing. Then I see the shore. In my boat, and with the more effort, I sail. I set sail, in the boat. I, am gliding across a lake. I arrive, to the shores. I, with my friend, cross safely.

On the other side, is the Earth's Heaven's, living, castles in the sky? I lived, a vision, in Young Life camp, of the "New Jerusalem." I saw my, Heaven! And, I am happy. I am just a man. I do not know how a man ever? I sailed, in a boat? I've, have had my visions.

My vision of my life, in this, is in what is, true as my Father's – "Friend!" Hell is within him. Shores on the other side, he carries himself, in the boat, to dry land. God wins, in my mind – "Jesus Christ!"

The America he sees beautifully is guaranteed his, as an ongoing life. His life history, form in the scenario from world war three, hates the worlds of hate. Here is the example, acting when this is, alive.

In and from, how I have fought, inside of the intellect of God, in the world, from wars. Schools, all over the world's people, have neglected young minds, and disregarded teachers. And the goal wins

in learning. Whatever is another mission, of what I
am in, is from how I, came from, a new, another
side, of war. Americans lose. We, in all things, and
in olden times, are lost, in the media. The losing of
American values, in whatever, is in war's mind, of
Christ!

All deaths, win, in what is meaningless. Life, is
not, everyone's good. Choices and opportunities in
America are for men, in the school systems, which
get us started in wars. I, see wars, with some of the
greatest people, seeking me out, as the winner of
World War Three. Was not that what, I was
promised, in this good life? What history, does not
know, is that war Generals, and are crazy.

As, life of, in a boat captain, and asks, what might I
asked not of his, then, he took his knife, and then
took his life. Sin, knifed everything, of winning
therein are not, worth living in, the one and the not
another situation, by the America soil. I, have
failed. I cannot mean, to lose, in a life's – war
situation. In my life, by and by, I lose an egg. That
egg is the life of me. That egg is scrambled.

In, whatever I am gliding into as in, one man. From
whomever, he is faster in war. Lands are his, then
made faster. If, I loved, in an American way, is it
the ending forever, for my life? War, is in these
opened seashores, and skylines of our country. I am
paddling toward, the ocean's edge, and Satan's war

of Hell. My hatred lives inside, too much thinking.
I, live in the traded life. One and only, America
only lost.

If only, I lived alone, then I would, in the American
tradition, dream the American dream, and make
American my home. I, love successful, people.
What make sense, in the homes of mine, am me. I
am an American homeward bound, to live in this
country. In the past, nothing mattered. "I love
America."

I've, lost myself once. In knowledge, who dared
from dream? Perhaps, toward the dream, living
consequences, is the third world war. His love is to
love a girl. If I, loved her. She is my, Miss
America, involving support, to her. I will hold her
dear.

I was my old girlfriend's friend, and a lover. But,
she was mentally, as an illness, was known to
happen to her, "mind". She was an outpatient
example at, an American mental hospital, known as
– "Hope." As, she fights to stay alive, I must not
protect and know her, she calls herself, but she is
mentally ill, at what matters in world war three.
Mass, I do not know her.

In the American tradition, of forgiving. Above the
skyline, I've, seen all kinds of people, in all ways,
of life. This is my father's land. I now cannot see

dead people. In this life, and in my last dying death,
I cannot, die.

This is because I have Jesus.

Life, as is promised, not to kill you. The meaning
of man is in the American. He, knows your life,
and your death's plans.

Hell he wins, how he can fight a victory war, over
you, and not, your happy lives. His, is United
States of war, calling. Understanding is in war. He
calls his father.

His nation is at home. He wins, and eats dinner, at
the same, kind of meal, with the same, kind of
people, as them. He, cares a lot, for the American
tradition, peace is so much harder to maintain when
you are high. The lands of America, from mine, are
what is the chosen lands of the promise of the war,
in the land of the free.

The home, of the American brave peoples, that I
knew is free, is home. I like, to call America, home
to, everyone. Wars are easy. If I start people, in
world war three's ideology, all then, for a people
win, a historic feat.

And as the forest's trees, hide. And, attitudes, on
the boat glides, and as the reflection of the crystal

castles, are what I stare at, and see, with a view, of Saranac Lake, New York.

My plan is to divide the American waters, with bad irony. I, have loved Jesus Christ, but I, always also loved, God much more! I have sailed the seven seas, wherein everybody is looking for something!

But as comes, what of nothing, but war, in my big life. I envision World War Two, like this, vision. In order to cross the shores and make it to the other side, I go across, wherein I go, and will go, swimming.

Nazi, Germany's Hitler's, becoming famous, came of war games. All wars were not war games at all, but examples of hate. Expenses in this free life, paid of queens living at the top, are not, worth this cost.

If I win, the war games from the top dreams, Jesus Christ, is in this life, as counted, then that is at all new world order. In, these expenses, pens are futile. The chosen lands, in the Holy Bible, were written of, by Moses!! He must win. He, saved the chosen, by parting the Red Sea. Water, is able to drown you, in the same way, that slavery is what, attempts to know, my God's, naturalistic nature. We are all, that which drown at sea, unless we are chosen, by the chosen by, History's God's people. What, if I am not? Life, in the land of the Promised

Land that as not in Heaven, does anyone ever drowns, but cannot is, by Jesus Christ.

Some ever enter ingoing, that never again, from the shores of America, will I swim alone, perchance. In world war, I am swimming. As I may never go to sea, I will, not go alone. If I, ever again, go to world war three's, I will be prepared. My America is due to Jesus Christ. He is life, from the shores, in a foreign land.

If I can seek the American gold system, to see myself, crossing the lake, then I am a homebound person. To cross, the lake is my greatest desire, in life. If I, want to be myself, as I see the things, in war, all of myself, is then going back and forth, to the end world, of the new world order, of America's. Waters high, not going overboard, of the showing of the darkened waters, in the crystal life, of the story's past.

The colored rainbow, is in the sky, where Heaven and Earth, combine sides, is from what colorful. Colored, from one shore of beauty, as hand and hand, life wins by crossing the body of water, to make it to the shore. Across the lake, swims all of your life, with another, able-bodied person. I swam, across the water, to the Kingdom of Heaven.

God knows Himself. The loved war has itself, a God. If He loved war, then the entire world would

be His. Life, fallen the same. And, from Jesus
Christ, in little times, came along, in friendships, to
lead the masses, astray. This is according to the
American people.

American empires were lost, in the olden days. To,
those who lived a life, I thank, every one of you.
The person you are measured by is seen in court, as
"always loved". For all, who loved you, as, my
Americans, and in life as mine, some day, I will
thank you, in the top-secret spot. Does, anyone read
the Holy Bible, from God? Must I respect your
choices? In world war, we are sacrificed as lambs,
in this frame, of mind to the USA, people.

Everyone, we all know about, talk about, how life,
and war enemies, can talk. They speak, of world
war's, plagiarism, in lost times. How the American,
intellect and, smiling faces, of the lost America, and
its everyday losses. We, lead over all, about the
life, of the world war three, from an American
perspective, of a natural war's leading, person. I am
an American President, and as a person, I can see
you. I can see all of you, and, then in this
knowledge, and what is seeing what, in the world is
about the world war three.

I am alive, in whose country, that this is about, is
into the, "Mad World." From the shores of the
Young Life camps, castles in the sky, I saw once, in
the vision of mine, where I learned to swim, into the

"World War Three," waters. I, have been, told that I, was a great leader. As one American, came to know an American mindset, then of itself, in knowledge of itself, who tries his hardest to win, wins all, and in this life of mine, what is takes, and the Antichrist, who it takes, to win world war three.

In America, the Antichrist's America, and what is about me in times, and what concerns that is about the Bible, is of God. I can know that the world war happens, overnight with the Illuminati's, army of darkness, and army of goodness. And, from the American Dream, is the Antichrist, coming of the new world order, in the age that is from evil men, compared to all, we all will win, with Devil victories, but not in this lifetime's dreams.

My life, then is good. I am elected President, in what I am now forming of America, and in the visions of the New World Order, comes world war three. I can see, in which comes truest, in the America, of mine, wherein this war happens. Overnight, war itself is going to happen. My life is in going to World War Three, all is going, to be mine.

In itself, and from my life, came the life, and in I believed in, the American, of "World War Three!" To demand in fact, about what is about these wars, in this book, that I win over all with, which is in from the writing, that is of mine. The real idea,

behind of the American dream, is in the
"Antichrist!"

America's whom is then going to war, to become
crazy, as the American people. To follow the
leader, and see what wins, we must follow the
Antichrist of America, to see life. Then the
America wins, in the third endings, of the third
times, of the third world war, of the third person.
The dream, of the American Antichrist, of wars
comes true, in the life chosen, to the wars.

I, follow war's denials, of that event, which is so
very crazy, that the situations, in how we react, are
even having world war three, which sees wars, as
the annihilation of the human race. The purpose
from this war, in the life of mine, is to become the
winner, as a winning part of America, as the war
itself, moves on larger attitudes, and covers more
land, than the previous ones.

The work from this book seems like a real story,
which is all for the crazy life, of the war. In a war,
in terms of Jesus Christ, there is a God, and a Holy
Ghost, in another war, of world war three. This is
because of America. He is the Biblical Antichrist.
He has a thought disorder, which tells us this story.
The story, came truest, of one war. He, is so evil,
that he is crazy, from the evil, even from Babylon of
the Holy Bibles. He is even, considered evil, by

God and Jesus Christ. This is how, the war was told to me, by my father.

In the End Times, there is one fact, in America, that is true. This is that there is a, "World War Three," and, it wins. The wisdom of one man is in the Holy Bibles, as a Bible verse. It warns, of the Antichrist, of the American, "World War Three."

The stories, and the new world order, can come together, to form thoughts, of the truest, kind of thinking, of man, in the kind of war, we all loved. The New World Order, that is always American, is in the "One Man", who is also in the Third World War, as its, "Leader of the Free World." He himself fights in the American wars, and He wins. And, to cut the hand off, from the arm, that is also, another factual existence, of war.
This all came, from the world wars, that all are in the Antichrist's America body, and in how the Great Prostitute, leads it. Inside Texas, from the city of Dallas, in the state of Texas, is a, world war three, amounts to people. He is the evil one person, of World War Three.

I came from, into what is in the makings, of the American dream, of World War Three, in Texas, and in the story's tales, it is us then, that wisdom explains. In the language's title, of this book, is for what as is the message being delivered, and in the ways, for the wars, we win, that are the inadvertently wrong way, as the message to the public.

In this life, of hopefully seeing war things, that come apart, as the story unravels, there is the one man army. The ideas are closer, to the end, as much as each penned man, in what is written, that has the joining problem, of one man, of World War Three.

The mind of God warns, of the Antichrist. In Holy Bibles, and in what are simple, as in the warring sides, of the wars, are in themselves, which are the ways, of the wars, of themselves. What, is meant of war, in what to all means, which life is from itself, in this life, from themselves, as war Americans.

When, data strikes the interception points of life, of the triangles, and then forms the wisdom of a man, then people win, strategically. Wars come from that which forms the philosophy of war, as is in creating the life deeds, of the war, itself of killing, in many different forms. Ways, of a soldier's life, and then from this march to the end, begins from Dallas, Texas, and then goes to where the grown men play, a war game. In Texas, in who wins over enemy warfare is what is involved, in the business, of war games.

What seems to be in this story, is the Antichrist, and was a young man, which I've met. In this life, I've liked him, and he sought fame, and glory in this life.

He was in the Dallas, Texas, part of the family that was at the party, of the Texan Wynne's, family.

I, am from the Wynne Clan's family of, four hundred members, in the – "Great State of Texas".

The mathematics are the strategy in my life, from the participant's life. His name comes, from a soldier's tales, and of madness. It is important, to know, that we win. As madness, there is as, war. Past the lands, of time, dwells the understanding, of one man. In, his USA, in this age, world war happens. He is the Antichrist. He is in Bibles. The world, of the American from the Antichrist is all for, himself. In the Biblical Revelations, he is one evil man. He, is not equal to the six-six-six, he carries, around on the mark on his head.

The man, who wins, wins after a cause. He must establish it, in the intercepting of deaths over wins, which is in, American life. That is the President, of the USA! His story is the best story. His life is important. It is the story-line. American deaths, only lead us, to time. Inside of lives, his winning lives, that is as, he speaks in tongues. He wills speaks, to the cost of man, in – "World War Three!!!!"

People, are like the damned, attacked civilizations that is in the, "Antichrist World War Three". The data, formed as lines from the interceptions, came when the wisdom, is of one man. He marched, and created all, of this life. Then, this was in the fall of man, from the kind of the "First Paradise", that was the – "Garden Of Eden".

The Third World War is not predicted, yet. We all, do not know history, of our world. In stories, all speaks of the Antichrist. The Bible, American Antichrist is the man, which is in these ends times. No one knows how he is to come. The person, sure of himself, is an American. World War Three is the war he fights. And, he is coming soon.

To endings, or the man of the Armageddon, of a world war three, is of just one man. He is coming from, Texas. The man who is living from the other men, is from our, "New World Order!" The one man gives orders, to all men. This is how, world war three, happens. He in the newspapers gives us all orders in America.

The one man, he is evil. America is marching triumphant. As the songs from the soldiers, made sense, we march. In, passing to safety, we win, the created life, from wars.

All came from wars. Life is in none of what I can feel. Mighty honestly, is in waging wars. Inside of the mind, what the war humanity, does. Losing, sides. For, in ways which cannot be intercepted, as losses, we win. Nonetheless the powers to be, unless, the day as the knowledgeable world, is accept evil, then all will lose. American lives in history, that soldiers marching, and going to wars, is heralded.

He, as God, came from all evil men, unless interpreted, in truth. We, form our actions, to be, what we are, "America's Public!!!"

As tried and true, no evils can accept man. In wars, no one wants, to win, from the intelligence mind's ways, of Communism, to be only from, the standards, from evil men. They come in from pirate ships, and destroy our nation.

The living wars in this life, within the evil men, are all of, "World War Three." Sand in eyes, explains why he and she, is evil, in this war. We, are that the triumphant soldier's march, that is of the Antichrist. If I, accept the American war, of third time, thus as the American President, I can explain this action, to duty. It is simply the fact, that from what America is, thus I wrote down on papers. Therefore, war as soldiers marching, is then in this book! I wrote down World War Three's, main strategy.

But, of it seems as if war, exists, than so do the killing. There is in mind, the souls of the lost, and innocent people. If at all, one day, we lose?

Would we, if this really was the true, war? My life

would continue on as the greatest. Only my version would be accepted. Heaven's Jerusalem, is the final destination, of this winning, from my acceptance, only in war.

Then, in hatred of a mad man, is alive. Lands of opportunity, of his vision came out. Golden trees clogged his mind. So now, he sees. He really, in this life, is not one of Americans. We learn, from the Holy Bibles, to serve. But, in that act, but himself; Adolf Hitler was this madman. He, is the example. We, have learned from, our past mistakes. Our wars, came from the common sense. We are of ours, as the Americans. We all, shall will, the wins, of our Country. And, then we would all, celebrate. In Christ, we who that wins, over all worlds! America, if now, as herself! She – could see? America, can win.

The Antichrist, or he, who in this life, wins over all of his wins? We all, win then. Third wars, of the world war three times, if in wins of ourselves, can we know justice? His anarchy, replacing by justice, is known through killing the whole wide-world.

With the wars of the worlds, phrases, and highest intelligence, all wins. Americans, can create the designed, of a circled life-form, that forms the shaped, loved deaths. The world war three, as the dying aged of man's victory, won. We are from deaths. They are the pasts, of the wartimes. The systems of wars, of the better man's philosophy, can enter! We enter a third time – "From Myself!" Americans, enters into world war.

Marching soldiers, into the unknown, rapes the USA! From national freedom, is the soul. Nations, of the world wars! Our versions are complete in the arms of America. War's soldiers, are those who end in the evil ways; lives of humanity. Then, this all, makes sense, to Americans.

The triangle death, and the circle life, takes shapes. "We are alive", to form illumination, in this, form today's wars!

Who in, the American world, sat and stood, one day? Who sees, from the world offices, a persons' big chair. Persons of – wars!

New World Order, wars, is personally growing as today! Faster and faster, onto the mostly thinner world wars, was what formed, a life. Will won, within the war's front lines. Me, as in what, schools created. By must, of what comes, the victory of the created lifelong victory's standoff, then wars of, all the wars, can happen to be, only America's, from Ancient pasts. We, wins.

The tree's life, with the ripe apples or oranges, is on trees. To, who lives a life, as an apple. It also dies from death. The supportive tree lives, as if, to please. And, when it dies, a person, can benefit. A tree, is for human, pleasure. That is to why it lives.

And whenever man fell, it was from the tree of life. The temptation, of the tree, was too much. As is, in wars!! As living is as dying, knowledge does, all. In trees, there lives life. In this tree, there came temptation. All knowledge, in war is, a cost. You, live either or you die, for what you are, is in how you can live, for your country. Why wars happen, due to knowledge, as in how came thieves, made from the form of Adam and Eve. The fallen world, was stolen, due to the disobedience, of one man, "Adam." All wars, of the greater designed natures; wisdom! Came, from Adam in the fallen knowledge, from the apple of death's construction!

Life of the wars, always in death.. The shaped and formed nations, came from apples. Wars came from what the followers, are to seek, in what is American. From past lifetime's apples, are the times ripe with knowledge? Actually war, is what an illusion, from knowledge is. Death of life, in what are designed from the wars, as from wars – "Is America!"

Thoughts of killing, is in life. Knowledge is as simple as the, illusion, as a tree. Whatever wins, trusted lives over are as is much, as God hated the Tree of Knowledge.

That is the reason, of the third world war. The double-edged sword protects the Tree of Life, in the Holy Bibles. The Tree Of Knowledge, came from – "Deaths!" That, was God's, curse on the human beings, from the life of the Garden of Eden. He, cursed us all, with death. That, is to why, all living beings, die.

The Tree of Knowledge was the tree of death. New deaths in wins, form as the appearance of God's will, as man fell. Cursed the world, from deaths from Adam! As all we stand, within circles, and the illuminated shapes, from the trees of life in forms of knowledge, came of the world war three's, soldiers, to die for our countries. The world will lose world war three.

Today, in that world, are what war three appearance of life, the fall wins, from knowledge. That is what, is in World War Three, caused losing deaths to other people. In masses, in what is from chaotic masses, we are as destined for victory! Lives lost and a life found, is what, came true, in death from the appearance of war. The natural selection, of the World War Three Office, of the President of the USA, costs deaths!

Three times, is the triangle, from one rounded, new world order? The circles, and squares, do take shaped, in this lifetime trilogy, of God's third world wars, entitlement.

The light within, in this guiding light, is life. The wisdom, can intercept what the living wisdoms, of prophets, can do and say, in world war three. The guiding shape, forming of new illusions, which can start now, can know questions of every, kinds of life. The book, is the simple explanation, that as from how, we die. But, to live, from the wars forming lives, from the Dallas, Texas, family? The three world wars, live in this illusion, in the story tales, of the fighting, in the New Jerusalem. God?

Welcome home to Texas, to the Great State of Texas, for the world war three's system, of the design, of the popular forms. The standards of wars, from one man to another whole man's catastrophic, versions of life, arrive to, the inherited in man. He, thus all came, for the Antichrist. He is this winner, from the war, as knowing the good and evil. Today is gone, from man, now and then, from what happens, to us. Watch me learn, as if the Americans, at world wars, were in the starvation of the planet; that comes in – "World War Three!"

These wartimes, that we know accentuate, what are the thoughts, behind the third world war! It is the intellect from America, behind the thinking, of a man. And the fighters of the war's thoughts are the very actions, from evil wars, of Capitalism. Natural ways that are not actions, but are in, these lives of the American Antichrist, of WWIII – extinctions

from deaths? But why are we living? Why, are
natures big to win, over all themes, over evil
winning in – "Antichristian America?"

What happens, from today's standards, of the
minimal costs of today? Why, in capitalist
designable standards? Waiting, from the
expositions, appear of life, in what is in the light of
the ways, of the exposure's lives, in the ending of
times, from wars, as all won?

Toward the seeing designs, from whatever is clear
intellect's, in what knowledge, from the mind that
the most people love, of these American powerful
families, wherein these choices, are from the
peoples, as to who finds out. What it, is intellect of
the unexplained. I knowledgeably can, alone can,
ever feel that I alone as myself, and me only, in
wars! What happened when life's happiness; lost!
I, never have fought; for all evils.

America, in what there is, must be a new age
started. Of one life, as all of the third time's war, as
first in what begins today? Now communism, in a
third world war, wins then from first win, and
continues, to all of their world war three's,
derivatives, that skills to win the war, are none.

Intelligence from our humanity's core is from,
living. American great slice of the American pie, is
how, America wins. This is, to the equality that

means nothing. If no life's edge, and in wars, to that meaning, as nothing is at equality, then in this life, death does win.

Apart from God, then enemies will lose, to the higher powers. All, of war, does win! Then success, and I and, "Ourselves," from our wins, will find intelligence, from wars. Intelligence from books, are the people from wars, and the wars and the lives, within hell, in what came from people which, we lost to.

We all lost battles, to the Holy Bible. If we do rely on Satan as our master, then America is, lost. How wrong! Why, in wars, would a nation, sell our soul? If, creating Satan, is the evilest act ever, we as Americans all must learn! He, always is our enemy. In the distance, farthest away from God, in the good people's loving life, there lies another – "one world order!" This time, it is warring sides in end days, in everyone's good America.

In war, of the churched living spaces, are the places of the God's interesting, and most loving people, who do no wrong, and do not follow World War Three. Following the hearts of Satan is known as, what are impossible. Into the measured distances to war, contradictions are from the problems, to account for dead lives, in the world wars, which are surmising. There is no future, with what is not, in what people's pasts, really are.

But, missions from what militaries want, is now as
world war, and but what is in the future's lifetime,
which does not matter, and does not amount, to
anything? We live, our lives as to live well. But
what really is in what the world war's, strategy,
really wins! Covering all peoples on every nation,
within all men, thereof, in counting the evil men's
plots and problems, against what, came as
American's, nations.

We as Americans? Why, are we not all equal, in
other countries? As Americans, we are in living
this life, which we are not all equal, in as a
contextual, life in happiness. In America though, is
a greatest force of the life, if there is no one of
American equality, then there is no fun experiences.
Life exists in, differences from deaths, which are in
the middle, of living freely. Do, not put death in the
middle, of this free-willed life, that sins in war. It,
will survive, on its own, like it never did, in the
enemy – Nazi Germany.

In three world wars, there are three nations of
elected and equal people! We are in wars! Now we
are all, as are God's, equals? Then, in the Trinity of
God, is the saving of souls. War's won worlds!
How sacred life, saves the souls, of the people. As
another form, of it! As, a war's third time, as an
office, in an office, I am a sad man! This only-
"War!!!"

Whatever, if what this man is, that the man is –
"Barrack Hussein Obama." The sadness, or enemy,
of this office, is that the Presidential Office, man is
– "World War Three!" We will miss your, life and
death; – "Mr. President Barrack Hussein Obama!!!"
We will now know, that love is war, and war is
loved. We will choose, a new American nation, of
American war-times, for nationalism. To wage war,
is to gain, allies!

My America, in world war three's, office! It is
excellence, in why that, is to the American nations!
Lives in what costs, is to win over all evil. This is
gradually, in this lifetime.

The lives, from the unknown, are simple
explanations, from myself. Warren Buffet, a billion
dollar man, is well worth; all. Trials, are insanity,
and are from what, angels do. Fallen angels, denied
happiness followings then mattered to men, is what
are too simply put down, as an insult to continue, to
be mine. The – World War Three, appears to be
mine.

All, in the Holy Bibles terms, are from – "the
Antichrist."

I've really literally, wanted to write in this book, to
be like the President of the USA, behind the notes,
behind the Cello, performing beautifully. Behind

the wars, there are always a political office, seeking out, the victories.

Our own thoughts, if I could war, be a won US President, from a war office, in sin. The sins from our fathers, in your American dream of war, makes us upon the hill of all, the seat upon the tops of the dollar, of the new world order, that reinvents itself. Followers, came into the followings of the new world order, and the, "Man of Sin," who wins, in that recruiting way, who recruits America, with private working, men of war.

I am, that in which, in followers, in wars, in which, arrived and came as himself, wherein I am – "The King of the New World Order." How history, lies in the senses, that I do care, from all the fights of the world, of the Americans, which were, made to be, in history's pages, afterward wars then, count me in, as I am, Riley Miller.

The world war's times, are exampled in the book, in what are the prime examples, as to what appears from life, as to be towards people, who begin to see, just are what is to a greater method, from war's madness. These shaped ideologies, to the formations of the front lines, of world war three, which are the asking from which is, Antichrist America.

The methods, from the "men of madness," came out
of the Texans, whom think of the American
philosophy that was foretold in Holy Bibles.
Americans, from the antichrist age, begin first and
last, as coming from life. The acts, from being in
occupied Bibles stories, from the American
approached circle of life, we'll win.

The standards of living, in one voice the greatest
meaningful life, is an American war, life. One man,
whom of which is, now! The Antichrist arrived into
Dallas, Texas. The strategies and plans, from the
war of the third world Texas, is of the third time's
wartime's life, and from firstly started versions of
world war three's death's construction, is what
book's were mine.

The lived as the extinct plans, of as all of the
people. The war's demising, has to be what formed
from the philosophy of the world itself. The one
American man, for the American self, of me, as a
complete as him in forming nations, is gone.
Always, Antichrist America, wins of the World War
Three demise, over China, Germany, and Russia.

The exampled life, from the thoughts, and
formations of the circled shapes, vie from victory.
These won wars, do not happen the world's way,
but from world wars, from the third time after Adolf
Hitler, we tried the American world war's times.
The example of winning and waging wars, of the

message, is not American, but anti-terrorist. Only from wars, is there no war, but from who is around the world, who supports it.

Go to the USA, of the world war three's coming, and find who, is the Antichrist. No one person, from the biggest American world war, can defeat him. He, came in the coming, from the peace of fame, in Bible's characters. He, from another wonderful war, that begins soon, starts as the bigger American soldier! Texas, then ends in the destruction of the whole world.

The life, within my dreamed, times ago, from the age of madness, is in a world, of present in times. As all repeating the history, I then purpose to the Great War's, no solution. The American soldier fights, again, and again, and in the world wars, carries life, on into the future. The, "Third World War's," theme of written works, is their, first and last, themed book. Books, of mine, are which is very read, and very popularly sought as in war, are the cleverly genius written.

Take careful notice for attention, in world war three's democratic state, in what is if consideration from the books is needed, pray then, what you read. In America, this is from God. In God's country, whatever you read in the books you choose, no matter, which chooses it, America wins. Books, also win. As, I believed in God for your country,

and any public person accepts it, we win together.
Always, if willing and able persons, can willingly
see, a be a part of, wars to be, then in the Holy
Bibles, is a powerful message of God.

The war's, generally made readers, won. Of this
book, from the history's living legends, like
Generals, Presidents, and World Leaders, of
whomever win wars. In US history, is an officially
new world order's book in the chapters, in what are
coming from what, is the instruction book. The
words are repeated, to strengthen you, and to seek
in history, what we shall find. History's pages
come from symbolism of old wars, which is in
wars, from only one man. From history's legends,
in which leading the USA's masses, and killing all
of the armies, of the other country, is the USA goal,
from the antichrist. How, then do they lose and,
then go away.

The circles of the world, with the war lines, are
soldiers around the wisdom, of man. He circles life,
of the worldly, craft. These wise thinking, from the
thoughts of man, exist to please God's wisdom, as it
is in and of every, "one man". All, American wars,
have been in the past life, and has been from what is
formed, in and around wisdom. That catastrophe is
wisdom.

Thanks to the reader, from the "new world order",
as an ancient order, can guide you to the truth, of

the followings, of the world war three. From wars, of all times, you will be interested. Examples follow through, in the lines that are reading, to us. These world war, are the wisdom and excellence, of what I have seen! The Antichrist of America, with all the nations of people, and as followers of everyone, I see in the vision, of the whole world? Yes, following parties, in the circled triangle, going into world war.

The actions in life, and of the dead, are of world war three, from what is from this book. Thanks be as, to all men, and of my readers. Wars, from what this Antichrist, as seen is, in as what takes, in American shape, what is from winning. The one man, circled in shape, as the "Tripled-Six." That evil man is that man, who starts what is this worldly war – "The World War Three." I am, to begin, to win in wars. Wars come from my life's greatest philosophy, of reading.

This is of the war, of people itself, seeing victory marches, in itself. The American man, is the Antichrist American man's lives, beginning to, begin supporting saviors, of the world. The human coded designed standards, is yours to keep, onto the pages, in this books. Not, only in my life, there is war. But, also in wars, if America lost, then the end of the world would happen. I am the believer, of the American tradition. If, the circled terms, we all fight, and American's armies, wins again, and again.

Riley Miller

Chapter 2 –
My War's Most Untied American Demands

War – Wins!
However in the United States of America, In It's
Lost Wars, Do Even Americans Win, Over All?!
Into, The New World Order, From the Totals of
Upper Constructs, in All the Costs, Of the Third
World Party, Come By the Word Of Mouth, And, In
What Comes From the Outsides – "The Third
World War's!"

From – "The Third American Nation's Wins"

Worldly People in First Ally, Of the Ending for
American Imaged Mankind.

My War

From the Biblically Antichristian America; We
Win!

We Come, All From the Unknown Soldiers, of
USA'S Pastimes –
In The Days Office's, Off The Presidential
Wartimes!

People Arrives all Over the Messages from the Holy
Bible's Revelations, At the Destined Predestined
Christians, And the Electoral Parties, Into the
Futures, Of All Wars, By the Elected Presidents,
From Them In Church.

Every Nation For The American President of the
United States from America, Enter Except Riley
Miller, Into Itself, in World War Three?!!

Why My National Ideology Of All-Knowing Peace,
Shared Actually All, But Nothing to War.

I Willingly, Accept the President Bid, From the
United States of America.

As Is, Another New Formed Ideology of the USA
World War's –

In a Front Office, War As Ways, From the Soldiers
Forming Lined Marches, To The Planning From
The American New World Order, of War –
America Wins These Endings From Times, Of the
Enemy's Status – The Death of Lives, In Peace

In Thinking That to Chosen Armies of Darkness
Rule the Global Elite, Then from the Willing Ways
of War, That All Is That Knowledge, That in
People, World War, Does Win!

What in Life Can becomes in the Surrounding
Areas of the World, from the Third World, Of
Peace? America, will win, and gain – "The One
World!"

Wars, that in Fighting, in the Status Quo, of the Americans who wins, as another new President's idea. He, can come well-enough alive, to start the official, World War Three.

If I Die, I Know When Entering into the Laws of Humanity, Then If We Should Be Respected, in the Destiny of the American, World! If, World War Three's People forgive me, then I am saved?

The American, Won All Over the Ways of Wars.

How in World Wars, Then It Is Done, In This Willing Point, To Be Of The Killing Of Innocent People?

Microsoft Word, From a Never-ending Plot to Rule the World, By the Antichrist. Is itself in, what is all to be mine, from all of mine, in the world war three's scenario, in society, of differencing?

I've, not knowledgeably learned, as because, of Buttered Toast, There Is None, Of One Duty, First Intelligent Only Leading World War Three In The Antichrist– This is But, One Country's Laws Involved, in Our Peace. If I Sell, These Are In These Laws, My American Man, When Has Every Soldier's Armed Units, and Then Allow There to Be Peace!

I am not the Devil's Advocate, of a person, who I am not like, in my life. I am, in the great looking family, of nice relatives, from the Wynne Family, In Dallas, and From Texas.

The Beast and The Antichrist, is in the Holy Bible. I, in how we have fallen, and fallen down hard, we can become, one world war advocate, in the wars from life. They are the soldiers, ending the world. The world is made by the, Devil.

Friends in this duality, and, in what was the intellect, came from laws, born in fear of each person, who is in charge of the ways, of my own, as life, or "the life," from humanity. The mind's approach, of the world, from over God, allow hands, that cast frowns down upon, on my destiny, to be this – "Antichristian USA"

In my life, and onto the world of wars, that if there are three wars, by one man who started one and finished one, to the ends of the American thoughts. Into, what it in war is, as the "New World Order", in what is from asked questions, if it is the way of the American, on top of these, top-notched ways?

I am of the new world order's ways into the days of every kind of everything which ends, but to fight in a war, is worth to risk your life for your country. The wars are in the days, of the tragic plots, and the losses, from one nation, of our nation, – "Our Nation!"

Confusion, about the started, "Antichrist," is of the, "God's Bible." I can know the things that are, way ahead of my time, and my publicly known image, and the places of vision, of where in this life, we are, there will be a world war three. Not one person can see, from my knowledge of wars, and what it is, within what God, has done, is a true life, to others, but in God.

Not even I can think as a person, as to think into the American dream. I am doing and saying, whatever another, man thinks, and, says in his life. In wars, there are failed, the war songs. These songs, that can appear, will appear. I can see the Antichrist, with the knowledge, of the "666". I can see now.

I am scribbling the messages on the chalk board. I am an attitude-adjusted, and a very special and clean, and sober person. I still can see and know how, of what I now know, and can hear of the overheard duty, and, as if ask it happens, then is when of the New World Order, if WWIII happens. If so, then Biblically, there will be Americanism, in the wars, of our home front in – "America".

How, the God's Holy Bible, in what came from my own creation, as in Riley Miller's, Holy Bible's version, of the last books, wherein the ending, of the holy books, "Accolades I & II," then all of revelations and from prophesies, and in visions, appeared in my NIV translation. The task at hand, in which is of a Holy Bible Book's remembered book, which has the versions of it, how of the versions, of the Holy Bible, in itself, in what has, from the ending of the books, of the Holy Bible, is God's Message, to the world.

The "End Times", in the Biblical Words of God, from the Antichrist, or "Son of Perdition", or the "Man of Sin", and a, "One-Man," ending the world, then it has war in the messages. In the Book of Life, and from the Biblical texts of old, that have inscribed money in it, and as an approving in God's message, there is the Word of God, which brings us riches. God knows, that from wherever, I've been, that is known, then He knows, even in what time night is, in world war three, even in victories, we will see, and to be, in these times, from World War Three, the promises.

These endings, of war, then is near, and is in world ended Biblical times, of the Holy Bible's, messages and the waging of wars, due to Communism, and of Socialism, and of the ideology in this America.

The "Anti-Americans," words in the believed in ideology, in from what the world's war attitude, will be like, as America wins over all. "If, I do well, I

can win World War Three." "Of mine, then is
yours, in World Wars." And, "All will do well, in
the Antichristian, "Three World Wars."

The Third World War, as to what is in America's
world, at this traditional life, that has life, in the
ending of all, and in wars. Seems as if, we can find,
and all people try hard, to find, themselves, in the
war of the end of the, "New World Order."

Then everyone, should beware, of this "triple-six,"
the forehead mark, symbols as the mark of the
Beast, and the Antichrist. The "tripled-six," is not,
on top of this forehead, but is in his Biblical mind.
The number, on this forehead, if we needed some
clarity, is what it seems to be, as pure evil. Ask me
how he, as seeking the number himself, from the
Antichrist, that appearing on our forehead, in life, as
we are controlled by him, and by the identity of the,
"Son of Perdition".

I, can in the thinking only of knowing and
cancelling of the doubt, and can have bittersweet
remorse, if I possess, of the Antichrist, it can be,
lived within himself. My living and breathing
knowledge from these times, I placed a halo, on top
of my head. Spiritually I was connected, to the
churches, to the alliances, and to the countries.

If I was, thought in my life, whatever I was
thinking, into the knowledge of the Antichrist, and

when of then his identity, as was occurring overhead, wherein I sat, we Think Of Destroys America! And As We Know Of American Life, And As the Savior of the World, Can Explain It, Of How The Man Or Tripled Six, is for my Starts, of World War Three!

And The End of America – "World War Three," is a new beginning in history. It does in fictions, the war and death, of times of trials and tribulations, in the end of the world, of there existed life, of the Antichristian knowledge.

We are people, at the third world war, where peace exists, foreign and domestic, of our America, of the Antichrist tradition. However in controls of the One Man's armies, in America, on showing us, the Antichrist, in what does the knowledge worth, dying and living lives for, ever attend to the new world order. Ourselves, in wealth from what I, really want, is and was, to have this, in this life, of wealth. Wartimes, should not only see, what won that is in American wars!!

Chapter 3 –
The Knowledge from War –

The laws of the Antichrist, as an approached to
explainable new world order, that as to attend to the
general unions, and the United States of America, as
for no one elemental doubt, and from arriving into
chaos, what happens is, in the end.

In that the new world order has some execution at
another, commanding situation over, another way,
therein is the American freedoms. What is, at this
life from whenever, in humanity exists in
apprehending the life's body, as it was, the
humanity killing.

What occurs, in the Biblical Antichrist, formation
from its only humanity that as killing is from and in
the name of God, if it is as American? The Biblical
Antichrist or one man's America, is in the adjusted
individual life's appearance, as an invisible
character, explains why chaotic meanings, can as
happened, at the shape of an annihilating impulse.
Why, does this happen, with in world war three?

The Leaders of the Bible to attesting laws, as wins
as leaders of the evil world, that people are into
World War Three, in God's world, as the Antichrist,
is Who Comes From The American Underground
Society.

He appears in the state of Texas. And acquired
intuition as applied, As the Attested and contested
to the explained moreover situation, is formed in the
knowledge, of the world way from the Texan man,
from what has in, as support in fact him of him, is
true war's blood.

His closed acquisitions, in which seems Of Another
Modern Day Stated Affairs, As Of The Official
Memberships To The New Aged Order, As The Old
Age, As The USA Itself, And Intelligence of The
One Man, Or The "Triple-Six," is now apparent in
America. He is the Better Living Human Being, in
attested form, on the world war grounds, From the
American genuine forth, of coming excellence.

The Founding Fathers of an American Antichrist
Agenda As Is From My Life As A Member of An
Official Group Of The New World Order – Known
To Only Be As The Brotherhood Of Death – In
However World War Three Will Be Won

The American Democracy's initially Stated Fact,
As Relied on the Secrets, Of The New World Order,

In The One And Only Fact, That The Antichrist
Wins, and the New Age Continues

Nationwide Treatment of the President Came As Of
The United States of America, Of The President,
Who Came As A Surmising Bold Win, Of WWIII

The New Appearance of the New World Order
Happens Overnight – Much Like The Treatments
Of The USA Americans, Who Have Learned To
Love To Lose

Freedom Will Carry On, As Unknown the Soldiers
of a New World One-Government Order Continue,
And We Won; The War!

The Presidential Questions Shall Arrive, Much As
The Stated To The Questions That Whenever All,
Over The World War Three's Victory and Arrival's
March, When Orders To All USA Citizens Shall
Start To Come, We Will Have Won.

As This Texan Times, We Eventually Wins! Then
We Will All, As One Will Be As Who Becomes
Prepared For World War Three, At Home

Then As For My Life, The New Aged Order Of
Faceless Mercenaries, It Will Appear In The
Doomsday Device Way, Known As The "Atomic
Bomb," Will Wipe Clean, All Of The Natural
Impulses and Make Clean and Ready a New Nation

With A New Chosen Population, To Undergo A
Change of Places, From "My Life!"

As History Known At Warred Universal War
Beings, At World War Three's Antichristian Ways,
Are In New World Order Warred Jews, Gentiles,
and Christians.

I'm Three In One, All Three In God, for World War
Three From The Trinity

Land And How The Senator's Powers and the
President's War Office of the United States – From
Them Knowing Already How To Protect Us All Of
World War Three

Of However In Life's Helping Hands, We All
Come, As Americans, While Others From Countries
When They Play Another Attributed Part Or Role,
As If In Texas, Ask In The Whole Lives, And Of
The Lands Of Freedoms

Who Wins Wars, From This Role Came Into The
Third World Wars, Of Trials And The Tribulations,
From What As Become As Independent And At
Intelligent Life From God, In The Triumphs And
The Victories, We Played An Important Life Part

I Began, As For Where As Whom In One We Win,
All Shall Win As The Trying War Games That
Happened To End Times Of All Over As, The

People In America That Do Things To Exist, We Win As One Whole World War

I Learned Life, From In How Life And How All Of The Americans Had To Come Together – Lands Even Had To Form Some Type Of Situation From Unity – And As Life When Discovered At The Soonest Times, We Ask An Overnight Underground Civic Question From Where Movement Happens.

 To Me– Then As This New Situation Occurs, Then At Split When This World War Third Time At The Third Time Arrived – What We Soon Will Be Safe And Sound Around, Is In This Life, From Ancient History

The Only One Rule Made Of Laws If Fullness To Appear – In Then The States Is Run By Individuals In Laws – From The Governmental, President Desk's Orders At This Time and Place Of the Desk – What Life Then Is Taken From The President's Chair – Takeoff Of the United States From The Formations To An Agreement – Made In USA Dallas, Texas – That To Mark My Words, "Another World War Of World War Three!"

This Third Times Of Christ's Life Means – Alone That World War Three Exists Towards The Status From A New America, As The Life From Independent Life Forms Exist and Endings, Can

Happen And Occur – And From The Jurisprudence And In Divergent Laws However, The Land We May Hold, In What Does Exist, No Longer The Laws But Of Freedoms

I, Can See That The Good And The Sold Souls From Another Ancient Aged Man, Is From Who Has, To The Modern Day Man, Of How An New World Oder Exists, From An Aged Old Order, Situation And From The Offers Of Another New Aged Faith Exists Into How Heaven Appears, And Exists –

This World War Is From However Texans Win, In The Whole Wide World Over And Over The Making From Man – From The Texas Traditions From The Overall Achievers, In the World War Three

In How To Win Over Allied Forces From Undergrounds Government Forming of Intelligence – Toward Protections Over All of the Global Elite, Thematic Events Of All Life, In My Plans of the Hidden in Secrets of the Service From the Spots Around the New World Order's Empire of Global Elites

To This Winning Of Wars – A Whole Deal From Antichrist America's National Approach – From the Plan From The Antichrist Escapism Philosophy of the National Interest Of The State Being

Annihilated to From A Happening Life's Coming,
An Evil Country, Of Atomic Bombs, in the Atomic
Age of Atomic Bombs.

To Protection, America Is Our Best War!   Idea
From American Supportive Interest From The Free
People, As An New Absolute Utopia of the State
I've Existed In And Have Seen, At What Has Come
To Civics, Or Of The Rights Of Everyone Of The
Human Race, As Liberating Beings, Our US Have
Fought In Wars. It Has, Already Been Days and in
It since One Day, When I've Asked To Seek God
And To See The Antichrist, He Will Nationally
Appear, Togetherness.

All Of The Allied Forces From American Systems
Of Designed Intellectual Interpretations, And For
The Forces Of England and All Darkness and Good
Sides To Win Over World War Three's Good From
True American People, There Are In Similar Forms
of Protection of the People, of the United States of
America's Government, Alive and Well.

The Past, History, In the New World Order's Ways
– Into Them Approaching From One Life There
Exists Movements From The Justice Protecting Our
System of Body of Warring Stated Allied Motions,
To The World Ahead In Its Life, Wherein At Life,
Therein Happens War

The Governmental Trying From Past Time's
Lifetimes Of American Learning From the Past's
Mistakes, of Israel and Allied Forces, Are Winning
World War Three Of Approach, To The Destiny Of
The People – On The Country Of America

Places We Go In Life's Wars – Nations and
Democracies, for the World War Three

People That We Meet In This Life – Can Come
From Places As To Where We Go – From Texas To
The World Table – Soldiers Eating The Blood Of
The Lamb – Sacrificial Rights For The World War
Three – Of Anyone's Lifeblood Made to Serve –
Gold Offers

New World Order Made To Win Over Every Person
- Made In This Life or Into The Live Of Mine –
How Everyone's Gold From World War Three
Planning to Remake Texas – Ideologists Who Make
The World War Happen – When As None Other
Than The Real God's Creation – The Holy Bibles
Made Not Of Hypocrisy, Then Are Introduced to
the World of War a Third Time

American New World Order (Sold In Offers) – To
Russian Communist Government – Lead By
"Vladimir Putin: If Lost Life" – A Former KGB
Spy- and a Russian Soldier of Fortune! USA,
Would Leaders, Will Entry Into, Killings of
Russian, If Corrupt In Homeland, Of Russia?

Vladimir Putin's Scandal – Madman with a new
Communist Manifesto – "New Order" – Like Adolf
Hitler, with his Nazis – Trying to Lead World War
Three With Extremist Scheme – Is the Bad Guy –
Who We Will Fight as the American Way

All of the World War Leaders Are the Perfect
Soldiers Toward – Their Lives Came From These
Adjacent Sides From Communist and Republic
Style Formations From the One-World Government

The History As The Same Ad Repetitions From
Two Times of Failed Sold Antichrist's Aged
Golden Offer to the New World's Order – The
News of Everyone Except the New World Order
From America's New Aged Systematic Trusted
Lives, A Deal As Agreed and Arrived at the
Conclusion that the New World Order Was the
Denial From Jesus Christ the Lord's – A New
Nation Comes From War – After the World Denial
of Jesus Christ

In Present Day – Already Happened – The United
States Presidents Sold Their Souls To A National
Cause – A "New World Order" of the Intelligent
Design – From A System of Capitalism To World
War Three, of Anti-Hitler Ideology, to Form World
Soldiers a Third Time with Justice

Leaders (old) Taught All Americans How To Fight
– A New World Order, to Form Overnight, After
the Precursor of WWII – All USA Soldiers To
Introduce An New WW3 – From Methods of
Practice and to, Warfare's Costs!

American Leadings In Times From War From How
- We Tried From Old World Wars, Three Forms In
Victory Over The Antichrist From America –
Unknown Takeover The World

Positions of Power From Men Who Ruled The
Globe From The Elite Positions Of The Power Held
Manifest In The Constitution of the USA

Places of Interests Won Worlds Over From Why
Men Fight From War's Glories

White Men's Themed Power Of Democratic Forces
From The Allied Government, of Dallas Texans

People In Charge Of American System From Its
Design

Presidents (new) Made In A New World Order
America From WWIII

Chapter 4 –
The Ultimate WW3 Plans of War

Parts from Plans
Whole Introduction
Middle Class Workers

National Leading Causes
Lands over Common Bond's Interest
Countries from Wars

Past Lives' Sold Souls
Present Ages from War
World's Past Times of Deals

Jesus Christ Is In Trinity
God Is In Three Persons
Holy Spirit Is God's Spirit Too

Americans Are the First in War World
World People Are Of Worlds
Plan of Action from Meanings

Buildings for Action
Towers To Command
Hideouts To Construct

Churches Of Worship Of The False God
Synagogue Placed Jewish People
Temples Of Designing Wars

Places In Life As Hurt America
Roman Temple Of Biblical Antichrist
Past Times From Aged Old Wars

Soldiers Fighting For The Cause
Areas Limited To World War
Plans Of Interception

Model America Fights
Club of Rome Secret Life
Parties of Political Deemed Acceptance

Saved Is Christ
Church Is Saved Regardless of Wars
Cities Plan Church's Remodeled Formations

Plans Of War Action
Cities From Hiding Out
United States Is Found In WWIII

Killing Is Deemed As Acceptable
Saving The Soul Is Impossible
Healing The Mind As Good

Nations Form Parties, Overhearing Justice
Democracies Create Philosophy's Endings

Countries Cannot Kill Presidents

Futures Of Past's Construction
Pasts From Denials Of Wars
Present Times Of Country

Times Of Life As Denials
Distances Between You and Me
Path Is From Distances From The War

Light In These Illuminati Circles
Way End's In The Pyramid of Gaza
Truth Is Wisdom Over Everyone's Time

Antichrist Is Made To Win WW3
America Is His Superpower
USA Won The War From Distances

Beautiful Creations From War's Succeeding Days
Magnificent Beauty Of Lights
Gorgeous America From Antichrist

Paths Of Forgivable Triumph Over Life
Roads From Paving The World's Lives
Streets Form Pictures From The Past Life

Police Cars Pave The Way For The Futures
Ambulance Drivers Are The Coming Home
Fire Truck Protects All Innocent Peoples

The Sections From My True Ways From
Knowledge Of Wars
False Life In The Mind From Man Verses Man's
Knowledge
Past Lived Knowing
As The Issued Pains
Of Other Life
Forms In The Universe

Sold Souls To Win Over Jesus Christ From The
Antichrist
Bought Life Asking If Jesus Christ Was A Savior?
Freedom as the Life Form of War's

America As The Solid Objection
The US Souls Brought To Freedom
Our USA Texas Family Wynne's

Country Made From Freedom
Land Is Our Property
Property Of American War

Fight For American Cause
Rights For The American Public
Liberties And Justices For All

Jesus Christ's Bibles
God Is Three-In-One
The Holy Spirit Lives Within Myself

Give Freedom The Chance To Win

Earn Life As A War Hero
Live Noble Life As Everlasting God

Fights Over Rights Of Individuals
Wars Won Over Evil Causes
Riots Occur Nationwide In Foreign

Live Lessons On The Power of America
Learn Life And Become Better Than Enemy
Know More From Life And Deaths

Animal Symbols Of Flags, Banners, Signs
Countries Signs From War Animals Representing
Flags Designed To Show Colors Of War

What Life Brings To The Table
How Death Knows Its Limits
Why USA Wins Overall

People Rights As Saved
Souls Saved In Eternity
Lives Earned Of Wars

Reasons Only Why War Wins
Examples From American Wars
Points In America Winning

Wartimes Over Americans
Battle Born Of New Prepared America
Fight Its All In The Tables From Presidents

USA Spirit Is In What Wins War
One Nation As Under Our God's Pledge
United People In War's Common Cause

Worth It All For The Wins Of America
Done Before Its Already Happening
Finished Already The Wars Ending

Stars Represent Fallen States
Stripes Cover All Over The Flags
Flag of USA Risen Americans Tradition

Soldiers to the End of the Worlds
Military Personnel of Government Figures
Air Forces Made In the Image of War

Guards In The Entrances Of Another World
Weapons In Wars Win Over Unjust Countries
Machines of War Designed To Kill Enemies

Peace Plans Came From The USA One-World
Government
War's Plot to End the World of the Antichrist
World At War From Fighting Old Wars

Intellect Known Over All of the USA
Mind Thoughts Occur From National's Identity
Imagination Does Do Right Things To Our USA

Hideouts To Keep People Safe
Base Camps Not Like Nazi Germany

The Planning Spots Like Hitler's Eagle's Nest

The USA Won Already
NWO As America Won
My Life Is Example

Secrets of the USA
Hidden Knowledge Places
Guarded Places of Secret Life

War Bombs
Weapons of Destruction
Atomic Age

Annihilation of USA
Destruction of Our Lands
Dead USA From War

Underground Books
Hidden Agendas
Plots to Destruction

Whole World At War (WWIII)
The Worlds At War (US)
The Wars of the World (Worldwide)

Freedom Idealized (USA)
Democracy Improved (USA)
Lands Free And Protected (World)

The Soldiers Fighting

The Machines
The Men

Fight For Freedom
Guard the Homeland
Make Safe The USA

No Terrorism
Anti-Extremists
Laws Against Aliens

Antichrist America
Biblical "666"
One Man

Starts World War 3
Misleads World To War
Leads America Astray

Satan
Four Corners of Earth
Kills Off Every Nation

Beast
"Revelations"
Enemy

Myself
Riley Miller
World Leader

Charmer
Gentleman
Leader

One Person
Two Leaders
Free & Sold

One Soldier's
Mind Control
Worships The Beast

The Story of War
The Plot Of WW3
The World War Third Time

The Third World War
The Third Time War
A "USA" World War

The Secret War
President of USA
The One Man

Stolen War's Office
Future War's Office
Past War Office

Made Money
Mad Expense
Huge Spending

Atomism of Spending Dollars
Expenses For Plans
War Money Plots

Laws Of Anarchy
No Protected Lands
Rights Of Life

Doom As Destiny
Antichristian Plans
Anti-American Plot Man's

Freeing of the Mind
Slavery Laws of USA
Anti-Rights (As Foreigners)

Soldier Protecting Homes
Foreign Laws
American Laws

Peopled Culture
Peopled Laws
Human's Rights

People are People
Rights are Rights
Laws are Laws

Homeland As Security
Laws Protecting Lives

Pro-Peopled For Laws

Free War's Land
Pro-action Wars
Free And Easy Laws

The USA War After WWII
The American War
USA War's End

Laws of War
Freedom of the Country
End of America

Storage of Food
War's Resource
Humanity's Natural Foods

Supplies to Help Maintain Desire
Food To Feed The Mouths
Resources of Natural Substance

New Order Is Old Plan Of WWII
New Age In Current Time Is Good
World Order Can Create WWIII

Foreign Protection For USA People
Homeland Guard Represents Free Americans
America Is War From The Ends Of The Earth

Antichristian America Fights Armies In WWIII

Anti-humanistic Laws Keep Sacred The US Mind
Anti-America Should Not Be Right

Find Plots Of Money, Gold, and Soldiers
Design For War's Plans and Plots Thicken
Humanity's Third End of the World We Live In

The Will To Power Enters The Picture of Antichrist
The Mind of Destruction Is Enemy Plot To End
Christ
The Heart of Design Carries Home Pictures of
Madness

Beauty of Vision Of War From Times Spent are
Valued
Boldest Plan of Free World, Is Designed By
Antichrist
Magnificent Fall of the USA Is Made To Be
Happening

The Hated Leaders Plot to End Good In Evil
Minded Laws
The Foreign Places Protected By America Is For
WWIII
The USA Wins Easily By Antichrist, And Force of
Its Will

One Man To Hell And Then World War Three Is
the Devil
Leadership In The Formation of Followers Populate
the Lands

Follow USA Is In This War, Idea and State, From
Annihilation

Spots of Plots Design the War Machines, Of Our
Nation's Arms
Plans for USA To Win, Made Possible, By The
Aristocratic Elite
The USA War, Spreading and Constructing, the
Image of A Man

Holy Church's Decisions, Is In The Bible, From
God's Elitists
Masses, Help Feed, Clothe, and Shelter, the
Misfortunate
America's One Man Is The Antichrist

States of Anarchy of the World's Diseased, Come
Cured
Protection of War Is From America's Decision, To
Die
Safety On Warring States Is The Savior of the
World Duty

Plotting Of Mass Destructions, Can and Will, Plot
To Win
Christ's Deformation, From His Crucifixion, Leads
the World
Destruction and the Demolishment, of the
Government, Is Untrue

Free Citizenship To American's Nationalism, Being
Approved
World Freedom, Spreads America's Message
Democracy's Laws, Enforced And Reinforced, Do
Never Exist

The USA Wins, In Freedom of the People, Who
Died For A Cause
The American Wins World War 3, Forging a Path,
To End Creation
The Entire US Won, And All Lost, To the World
Order

The Wins of WWIII Of One Man
Land From Leaderships, Arrive From USA
Homeland
Wins Evil No Longer, Defeated By the Good

Good World, Carries Home All War, Freedom
Fighters
Evil Wars, Against the Good of Peace, Construct
Anarchy
Freeing Win, The Human Valued Cost, To The
Valued, Saved Model

War Song's, Decreeing Method, Risen to USA Top
Window Viewed, Over All
Desires, Around the Circled Man of Sin, Can Be
Carried On, Too Long, For Win
Meanings, The Antichrist Makes, Is Valueless

My Country, Is The Song, Repeated, As If It Was
WW2 Unto WW3
Americanism Is The Song, That Fights All USA
Wins, Of Other Countries
Homelands of America, Then In Fighting From Our
Freedom, Wins By Its Choices

Targeted Enemy Awareness, Counts Up Bid, Until
the Antichrist Comes, To Earth
War Time, In Losing Countries, Means That
Supplies and Goods, Are Valued As The Least
World Good, And My Humanity, Is Not
Overvalued, In World War Three, In Beginnings

Man of Lies, Who Cheats, Destroys, Kills, The
Status Quo, of America In The End
Deceiver Means No Good, Who Denies Works,
And Satan As Good, Deceives All
Satan's Person Is In WWIII, Who Is One Voice,
One Mind, And One Person (A.C.)!

Biblical and Churched Peopled Masses, Are Saved
From Sins, Who Lose By War
Christ's Following, of His Body, Replaced By The
Messes, The Olden Past Has Made
Followers of the New World Order, Are Counted,
In The Act and Deed, For The USA

One Person, Can Win World War Three, By
Believing In God, And Going To Church

Triple-Six, Is The Mark of the Man, From
Envisioned, Parts of the World, He Controls
Man of USA's Intelligence, Made The Man Of
Lies, Into A Condemnable Unity Of All

Know Enemy And Face Of Nation, Arguing Over
Lands, and Skies, In the Wrong Way
One World of the USA, In One Fact, Is That The
American Nation Is Protected, From Hurt
Triumph USA, Over The Laws, Of The Land, Keep
Out Foreigners, From Open Entering

Fears To the World, Came From Phobia, Of the
World, That It Is, Lead By Evil Makings
Safety Of Our People, In Lands of God's Freedom,
Except the Enemies, Of Communism
Person, As The Americans, In This Life, Has Been
One Man, From Ruling the World War

Philosophy Is The Act, and Deed, and Mark, of an
American, When He Thinks Alone
Killing Is As Certain, The Privilege From War
Beholds, Accepting the Wrong Way, Of An Man
Justice, Is the Position of the Laws, Into the War

Man's War Came True, And Lost and Won,
Everywhere In The Warring World
Home Win Are Family and Friends, Winning A
War Alive As Ourselves, In Victory
Lands of Freedom Are Designated, As Roles,
Citizens Play, To Enter Into The USA

Heart Is Made, And Controlled, By The Wars, Until
It Is Freed, Of The Victory Wins
Enemy Of the World, Is Any Anti-US Victim or
Oppressor, Winning By Desire To Lose
Killings Acted Out, In The Measured Worth of a
Person, In Life Founded From Our Lands, Can See
Heaven, From National Duties

National Land, Is Our Forefather's Country, That
We Protect, As Your And My, Land
American Land, As Of Soil, Could Be As The War
Dictates, That What Is Won, Is Won
USA Soil, Agreed With By The Government, As
The Person Directed, Are Agreeable Won

Conferences in The Life From Businessmen, Could
Hurt And Harm, Any Individual, In War
Meetings, Are For Meetings, Wherein People, From
All Over The World, Are Safety First
Rooms, Of Our Design, Are There To Help Protect,
All Laws Of Our Nation, Under God

In Secrets, Of the American Values System, Into the
Motion and Duties, Of Our Great Land, We Are
Innocent
For Production of American Values, The Trusted
Side Always Wins, In Good Ways
Talks, From the Old, And the New, Can Enter Into
Thoughts, In Appearing Doubts

Enter, To Heaven, and Leave To Hell, If You Want
To Play, War Games, With Its USA
Leave the Door to War, As an Adventure Open, To
the Public of the American Ways, Win's, The
Minded Games, Of American Soldiers!

The USA's Religion, and in the Christian Church,
Peace and Good Things, Bring One Closer To God,
In the Church

Decides of the Fallen Empire, of Ancient Rome,
There Were Choices, Of War That Made Them Fall
Fights Over Disputed Lands, Are Chosen From
USA, Property Of Our Mind's Eye, All As
Protected
Intelligence Is Thought Of, Well-off In The United
States of America's Presidency, Especially By Us –
All!

Open Wars Meant Abolition Of All Human Rights
Best Minds Works For Philosophy
Closed Minds, Are Ignorance

Selections, Of The Property Of The "USA's," How
Minds Control The World
Peaceful, Communities Entrance, Into the World Of
The Idea, Of Life
Community, As The People Involved, Harm and
Hurt, The Democracy, Of The USA

Battles Are Life's, Great Choices

Births, Happen When War
Death, Is Alive, In God

Generals, Are The Actors, From Another War's
Times
Presidents, Are Leaders, Of The Chosen Faith, In
The USA
War Leaders, Believed In Their Country, To Fight
Enemy

Planner, War
Decider, Fates
Plotter, Destiny

Americans Who Win
One War Has All Americans
Citizens Are The Good People

Church, Decides
Chapel, Surround The Soul
Bases, Control Points of Duty

New, Begin World War Three
Old, Repeat World War Two
Secret, Stolen Lives of WWIII

New American People, Actions Are Great
Old Allied Forces Put Together Lives
New American Forces, Won Together

I Win, Over Evil

Peopled Win, Over American Nation
American's Wins, Over Slavery

United States of America Wins All Wars
Foreign Land of Killing at the USA
Lands Won, Protect the American Public

Enemy, Of The Foreign Lands, Is Communist
New Order, Is Movement of WWII, Communism
Party
Communism, A Gathered Idea That Can Not Work,
And Is Evil

Sold, Government of One World
Bought, The Presidential Candidates
Fought, In the War Yesterday

Philosophy, The Movement of Greatest Thinkers
New Aged Order, Succeeds
Books, Tried and True, From Myself

Freedoms, Democratic Idols
Callings, God's Answer
Orders, Are All Good

Laws, Determined
Bylaws, Decided
Legal, Courts

Courts, Justice
Caste Laws, Heredity

Ranks, Followed

System, Government
Followings, USA
Democracy, Popularity of Presidents

Illuminated Ones, War's Illuminati
Idea, Knowledgeable
Christ, God

Army, Soldiers
Wins, War
Soul, Sellable

Legal, Represented
Illegal, Unintelligent
Record, Documented

Peace, USA
War, Foreign
I, Me

Sold, New World Order
Bought, WW Plans
Purchased, Three Orders

Poor, Lowly
New, Founded
Family, True Life

Budgeting, Money

Fees, Collections
Signatures, Identity

President (USA), The Whole New World's King
Final Judgments, The Last Ends of All Worlds
World War Ending, Judgment's Day Is Here Soon

Life, Lived At America's Deaths
Deaths, Death from Life Is Not Alive
Cost, Counted In Days 'Till WWIII

Pen, In Hand To Sign Laws
Hand, Cursive
Agreement's, Signature

Intellect, Mind
Mind, Thoughts
Attitude, Christian

Evangelist, Pastor
War, Worldly
Backer, Supportive

Finance, Dollars
Money, Financial
Ending, Statements

Alliance, Old Wars
World War, Third Time
Agreements, Settled Issue

Killing Ceases, World Peace
Friend Agreements, Negotiations
Superpowers, War Machines

Hot, Burnt
Cold, Frozen
Lukewarm, Hearts

World, United States
War, Enemies
Third, Numbered

Past, Old
Now, Immediate
Future, Light

Call, Beckon
Summon, Cometh
Believed, Knowledge

Triple, Deaths
World, Hated
War, Sought

Everyone, All
Everything, Itself
Everywhere, Overall

President, Elections
Official, Profile
War, Evil

Chair, Leader
Office, Highest
Leader, Powerful

Time, Moments
Chair, Supportive
Presidents, Chiefs

Deal, Agreements
Man, Person
Staff, Collective

Oilmen, Richest
Money, Making
Costs, Spent

Man, Alive
Deed, Works
Price, World

Sold, Itself
Pen, Signature
Paper, Medium

Forgive, Sorry
Press, Followings
Media, Coverage

Coverage, Overlord
Public, President

Person, Humanity

More, Above
Less, Lowly
All, Itself

Life, Living
Learn, Deciding
Brains, Minding

Pen, Agreements
Paper, Valuable
Golden, Sought

Weights, Strongly
Influence, Design
Decision, Remarkable

Hot, Rooms
Cold, Outside
Middle, Pathways

Missile, Atomic
Bomb, Nuclear
Annihilation, Extinction

More, Above
Less, Lowly
Monetary, Collectives

Start, Beginning

Finish, Ending
Middle, Undecided

Home Land
Legendary – Lives of One Man
Pay X-Generation Money

Fares At War's Ending
Benjamin's Dollar, Signed
Money,

Ben
Jeff
Sally

America
People
Trust

Deal
Decide
Pensions

Dollar
Dead
Presidents

Sign
Contract
Signature

Not
Yes
Handshake

Deal
Soldiers
Anybody

War
Peaces
Agreements

Person
Guard
Ideas

Power
Plans
Bombs

Rights
Law
Order

Victory
Reach
Succeed

Troubles
Ending
Battle

All
Over
Destruction

USA
Homeland
Outreaching

Cold
Desires
Soldiers

Noteworthy
Surprised
Legends

A.C.
War
Death

Lasting
Friends
Country

Religion
Laws
Soil

Final
United States

War

World Of The Third War
Globe Is Intact With Enemies
Whole Map Of America

Succeed In Armies
Knowing US Constitution
People Are Saved

Living In Texas, For Family
Dying For Nation, Armies
Learning The Methods Of War

Lifelong War Parties
Jews Of The Torah
Biblical Countries

4 Corners Of The Earth
Satan Is The Deceiver
American War In Texas

Whatever
Brought
Warring

Relived
Won
WW2

Third

America
Final

Three
Start
Finish

Evil
Good
Neutral

Top
Bottom
Middle

Lead
Follow
God

Win
Lose
Failure

Promote
Savings
Followings

Peaceful
Sold
Philosophy

Old Aged
New Aged
Present Ages

Sold
Idea
Teach

Fails
Loses
Wins

Billionaire
Backers
Financial

Produce
Find
Go Forth

See
Learn
Hear

War
Deaths
Killing

Go
Forth
Preside

Look
Know
Run

Seek
Find
Yield

Products
Flow
Rankings

Top
Spot
God

Hate
Life
Examine

Top
Spot
Known

Resources
Money
Billionaires

Raw

Material
Resource

China
Russia
Germany

Meaning
Leader
Rules

Highest
Life
Tops

Lesson
Learning
Products

Wars
Godly Man
Army

Golden
Money
Supply

Bank
Hideaway
Safety

Find
People
Churched

Little
Big
Wars

Bad
Evil
Good

New
Order
World

Light
Caves
Outside

World
War
Three

Want
Knowing
Plots

Evil
Wicked
Vile

Raw
Element
Materials

Human
Color
Races

Life
Deed
Rights

Story
Tales
Victims

Wrong
Right
Middle

Wealth
Money
Classes

World
Wars
Third

I
NOA

AIC

One
Man
War

Sold
Buys
World

Cured
Disease
Schizophrenia

High
Low
Middle

Class
Society
Culture

Fort
Bunker
Door

Today
World
Three

News

Medias
Press

Private
Secretive
Hides

Modern
New
Present

Called
Summoned
Life

Summoned
Believed
Known

First
Second
Third

President
First
Beginning

World
Spread
Omniscient

Planning
Reading
Finality

Plots
Plans
Product

Universes
Little
Highest

New
Old
World

Around
Planned
Age

Knowledge
Christianity
Order

Pen
Paper
Purchases

Seek
Worldly
Wonders

Home
Returned
Front

Reach
Total
Outside

World
Wide
War

Stop
Height
Place

Work
Action
Knew

Stops
Ceased
Exiled

Oldness
New
Ordered

Buying
Selling

Finance

Buy
Sold
Knowledge

Brains
Banned
Police

Kills
Deals
Society

News
Old
Sellable

Hot
Cold
Newness

Buying
Powers
Limited

Intellect
Powers
Limited

Intellect

Powering
Foretold

Sold
Buying
Finality

Sanity
Insanity
Mediums

Control
Mind
Number

Three Sixes
Forehead
Wrist

Beast's
Antichrist's
Satanic

I
NOA
NO

New
Age
Ordered

Sold
Souls
Desires

Big
Small
Medium

Noted
Pensions
War

Bank
Profits
Spent

Fortitude
President
World

Spending
Earnings
Allowances

Spent
Dollars
Sense

Plans
Peace
Wars

Top
Hideouts
Controls

Peace
War
Plotting

Spots
Hideaways
Secret Spots

Old
New
Camp

Wealth
Abundance
Life

Times
New
Olden

Days
Dates
Hours

Names
Position

Success

Gold
Silver
Bronze

Ends
Spending
Begin

Going
Out
Places

Militaries
Soldiers
Armies

Hate
Pride
Goings

Lens
Sight
Seeing

Philosophy
Perspective
Viewpoints

Doubts

Faithful
Reliant

Friend
Foe
Accomplice

Polices
Enemy
Crimes

Poorest
Richest
Millionaires

Power
Ability
Rights

Power
Nothingness
True

Sellable
Bought
New World Order

Matters
Truest
Strength

Highest
Most
Offices

Strongest
World
Wars

Nothing
Sent
Gradual

Peaces
World
War

Offices
Government
I

One-World Government
Fed
CIA

Five Most Powerful Men
Philosophy From Wars
New Order Of The Ages

New Order
Enemy
Communists

Party
Vladimir Putin
Political Leader

Academics
Learning
History

Pasts
Wars
Wins

Old
Offices
Repeated Officials

Identical
World Wars
Three of Them

State
Higher Power
Officials

Highest
Politics
Highest Point's

World War
Three

Vladimir Putin

Presidents
Past Offices
War's Politics

Russia
China
Anti-USA

Myself
My Office
President

Cold
Hot
Measures

Love
Hated
Relations

Find
Lost
Leading

Leads
Leading
War

Officials

Pasts
Presidents

Lovers
Haters
Doers

Hurt
Help
Goodness

One Cause
USA
One Man

Foundations
Nationality
Solid Rights

Research
Finding
Discovery

USA
WWIII
I

Books
Discussions
Plans

Won
All
Yesterday

Perfect Leader
Angry Man
Man of Reasons

Treasons
Faces (Many)
Identity

Treasured
Sought After
Known Evil

Antichrist
America
Person

3-6's
Animal
Beast

Armageddon
End Times
Apocalypse

End of the World
Numbered

Days

Counted
Lives
People

Games
Lives
Followers

All
Nations
Followers

Nations
World
Antichrist

USA
Everyone
Blindly

Few
Many
Forced

Smartest
Dumb
Realized

Works

Counted
Rewarded

Forgiveness
Sorry
Innocent

ID
Mad
Sorry

Identity
Bar-Coded
Mind

Controlled
Readings
Forceful

Brain
Forehead
Mind

Controlled
Purchased
Slavery

Triple-Six
Thoughts
Forced

One
Person
"Man"

Bible
Antichrist
"666"

Hell
Afterlife
Doomsday

Entrance
Eternal
"Satan"

Real
Official
Identity

Found-Out!
Realized
Defrauded

Decoded
World War III
Antichrist

One Man
America

USA

History
Living
Final Days

Judgment Day
Jesus On White Horse
Ending of Earth

Bad
Evil
Hell

God
Right
Heaven

USA
Riley Miller
Identity

Righteous
Heavenly
Angels

Rebellion
Satan
Heaven

Fought

Won
Fell

War
World
Three

Plus
Minus
Middle

Ours
Land
Everyone's

Free
Laws
Lands

Song
Dance
Rhythm

War
Treatises
Appointing

Minds
Body
Humanity

Personality
Classes
Hierarchy

The End
The Antichrist
The Apocalypse

WWIII
WWII
WWI

Happy
Flourishing
Better

Wins
Victory
Success

Black
White
Clearest

Forehead
Arm
Hand

666
One Man
Beast

Nothing
Clearness
Void

Darkness
Intelligence
Wonder

Light
Cave
Chains

No
Yes
Definite

Either
Or
Singular

Win
Lose
Void

Know
Think
Action

Tanks
Aircrafts

Boats

Jets
Pilots
Sailors

War
Declare
World

AC
USA
All

One
Nation
War

One
World
War

Repeat
3rd
War

Private
Public
Information

Economic

Government
People

Constitution
Bill of Rights
Emancipation Proclamation

Treatise
Documents
Handshakes

Church
Political
Speakers

Rules
Serves
Democracies

Worldwide
Wartimes
Three

President
Staff
Vice-President

Officials
Dignitaries
Magnates

Importance
Officially
Beneficial

Pro
Positive
Support

Life
Success
Gaining

Wars
Battles
Fights

Fright
Fears
Courage

Made
Decided
Attempt

"Pro"
"Con"
Declined

Jointly
Chiefs
Staff

Meeting
Gather
Socialite

Matters
Choices
Decisions

Walk
Fly
Ride

Strongest
Mind
IQ

Man
Person
Numbered

Decided
Chosen
Marked

Ordered
Newness
Worldly

I
WWIII
Light

Idea
Forehead
Number

Idol
Bible
Evil

Man
One
All

Evil
Good
Mark

Evil
Goodness
Liberty

Causes
Effects
Celebrated

Wars
Winning
Sides

Killing
Vision
Innocent

Murdered
Shot
Overpowered

Life
Persons
Allegiance

I
WWIII
AIC

Books
Manuals
Textbooks

Strongest
Smartest
Smarter

America
Russia
China

Survival
Contestant

Winner

Biblical
Antichrist
America

USA
Wins
Challenges

Presumption
Guessed
Factoid

USA
Wins
WWIII

Americans
WWIII's
Kills

Place
Date
Time

America
End Times
At Hand, The Hour Is

Evolution

Warfare
Survivors

Weakest
Strongest
Powerfulness

Kings
Nobility
President's

Soldiers
Fighting
Constructions

Remade
Pre-chosen
Fittest

Dallas
Santa Fe
Oxford

Texas
New Mexico's
England

Street
School
Independent

Smarts
Skills
Ability

Testing
Scoring
Learning

Perhaps
Maybe
Decidedly

Skillfully
Planning's
Masterful

Deadly
Alive
Living

Killed
Lifeless
Shot

Murdered
Killed
Assassinated

Laws
Rules
Legalities

Known
Popular
Famous

Readable
Plausibly
Scorings

Report
Documents
Treatise

Taken
Seized
Victorious

Class
Status
Report's

Social
Economic
Philanthropy

Hired
Recruited
Support

Earth
Planet

World

Decreed
Pronounced
Determined

Trains
Cars
Planes

Badness
Good
Reliable

Occupying
Seizing
Takeover

Terrain
Nature
Territory

Pride
Satisfaction
Agreeing

Homes
Offices
Workplace

Schools

Hospitals
Prisons

Lands
Freedoms
Democracy

Idealism
Fictional
Imagination

Party
Republican
Each

Party
Political
Past

Newness
Recruited
Followings

Ability
Purchase
Directedness

Belief
Life
Change

Old
New
War

Sold
Deformed
Tarnished

Lives
Hearts
Souls

Home
Work
Schooling

Three
Time-Span
Knowledge

Sided
Party
Slummed

Soldiers
Military
Fighters

Recipe
Information
Selections

Articles
News
Papers

Popularity
Gossip
Slander

Local
Distance
Nearby

Tops
High
Peak

Lands
Freedom
Fought

Smarts
Perfect
Skill

Targets
Groups
Grounds

Philosophy
Debate

Questions

Soldier
Kill
Save

Man
Antichristian
Human

Alive
Dead
Chosen

New World Order
Alliances
Old World Order

Banners
America's
Ownership

Saintly
Sinner
Freeing

Water
Food
Clothing

Adventure

Protective
Defending

Psyche
Atlas
Crazy

In Wars
Dialectical
Deranged

Promoting
Killings
Badges

Love
Neighbor
Peaceful

Attitude
Aggressive
Respect

Bodies
Training
Welfare

Pastors
Sermon
Death

Medals
Brave
Courage

Intelligence
Most
War-Times

Heroism
Activeness
Ranks

Plotting Points
Control Worlds
Decide Plans

Amazing
Structures
Capability

Winners
USA
Greatest

Duties
Saved
Lives

Great War
Unified
America

Glorified
Attributed
Adventures

Three Six's
One Person (Man)
Beware a Man

Duty
Active
Committed

Called
Service
Manhood

Holocaust
Relived
WW2 Of WW3

Predictions
Destruction
Humankinds

Visionary
Antichrist's
Following

Every Nation
The Triple-six

All Of Everyone

Warring
People
Following

The Antichrist
The Three Sixes
Mark On Forehead

Third World War
Freedom
American's A.C.

Win The USA
Over All The World
America Sole Nation

Everyone Following
Everything Controlled
Everybody Marked

USA President Obama
Watches Carefully
Role As Entire US

Killings Acts
Brotherhood Fighting
Soldiers Dying Forever

Washington, D.C.

Control Person's Desk
Presidential Control Point

Love Thy Neighbor
Birthed USA
Plan of Antichrist

Bombs Foreign Land
Attack Anti-American
Foreign Annihilation

USA's Whole World
Reconstruct USA
USA Wins Over All

The Club of Rome
The Societies of Places (USA)
The War Recruiting USA

War
Easy
Hard

Demands
Constructing
Buildings

Natures
Man
Animals

Rights
Places
Interest

Decisions
Leaders
Presidents

USA
Worlds
War

Warring
Level
Wins

Today
Now
This Moment

Wherein
Whatever
Wherever

Why Not?
Reasons
Causes

Wartimes
War Spots
War Places

Duty
Plans
Calling

Duty
Place
Things

Followings
Duties
Positions

Persons
Protect
Planet

Heard
Times
Productions

Times
Proclamations
Around World

News
Callings
Built

Persons
Duty

Called

Americans
Native USA
Productions

World War Three
Playing Fields
USA Citizens

Perchance
Directions
Aims

Spots
Protection
Hearsay

Gathering
Plans
Citizen

Build
Freedom
Plans

Democracy
Party
Republicans

Party

Followings
Reasons

Clubs
Societies
Memberships

Fellowships
Research
Willing

New Age World
The Order
New World Order

Persons
Places
Things

Events
Persons
Places

Chapter 5 –
The World I Made

Hard Times   American Wars
Useful Things   Society At Large
Philosophy Of War
States of USA   Places In World
Direction of War
Foreign Lands   Dire Needs of USA
Places of Plot
United States   Foreign Nations
Demand of Needs
Far Away Lands   Up-Close America
Places
United States   Russians
Foreigners
China   Germany
Localities
Allied Forces   United States of America

USA WAR!
Third World War
Destined Into World
Will Come In Time – Due
USA Will Win Everything

Antichrist America!
To End The World – In War
World To Come – USA Victory
Prophesy In Bibles – End Times

Apocalypse – WWIII

World of Fear In America
Will Wipe Out Everything
Comes When America Ends

World War Plots!

Construction of a New America
Rebuilding of Roman Temple

USA'S Wars!

Supply and Demand For Goods
Resources of Needed Materials
Energy From Resources In USA!
Top Soldiers & Armies Brought To!

USA'S Peaces

The Generals and Presidents Protect USA
The Men at War At Home Seek Good
The Supplies Are For War and Peace
The Peace of America Is At Home

American President

The Elected President Is For WWIII
The Vote For Office Makes Him Elect!
War for Him, Worked For Good
World War Three, Is Inevitable.

The War Effective

USA Is Homeland
Foreign Is Unprotected
Free Lands Are Good

The Peace Effected

Love is a Common Virtue.
Peace is not at all, of wars.
World Peace, is Impossible.

The Man In USA

We Make Our Own Choices.
At War, We Come Around.
The Man Is War-Based.

The Home War

The USA Is Protected!
No One, Can Destroy It!
America, Is Made To Be, Of Mine!

The Mind of America

Intellect
Mind
Imagination

Inspiration

Success
Life

All Three

USA Wars
USA Peace
World War III
Inspired Intellect
Freedom of Minds
The Reason Of Life As Too Much!

My Life

I, have habits. I, want to live, WW3.
I am depressed. I, do not love, life.
I have a reason. I am only a person.

WW3!

Soldiers
Payments
Satisfy
Home Front
War's A Nil
Impossible

Nothing
Something
Any Wars
No
Yes
Every War

Nations
Armies
World
War
Peaceful
Studied

Not
True
Biased
Fulfilled
Promising
Planning

Intellect
Machine
Superpower
Planning
Ideology
Americans

America
World
Third War

American
Gentile
Believers

Wars World Won

Pasts
Now
Kings
Won
Lost
Wartimes

Futures
Now Is How
President
Today
Purchases
Losses

Old USA
Kingdoms
USA Won
Emergency
Estranged
Topicality

New
Free
Won
Americans

Today
Alive
Fortune
Dealing
Empires

War's Won
Alliances
Newspapers
Pastimes
Present
Changed

The All-About America!
How America Wins WWIII!

Learning lessons, on killing.
Knowing America is innocent.
Trying hard, to know blamed.
To forgive, for tragedy.
To see the USA, in better ways.
Mistakes, are made to remake us.

Why Riley Miller Loses WWIII!

The Lost.
The Confused.
The Damned.
The Blamed.
War Calling.
War's Enemy.

WWIII Aliens.
World War Loser!

Lose Or Win?

Lost America, Means Nothing To Me.
Won America is, my life as good.

"USA'S WW3"

Feel Better.
Know Enemy.
Inspire Friends.
Counsel Brothers.
Win All Over.
Trusts In Oneself.
Treat People Well.
Seek First Good.
Correct No One.
Be a Happy Person!
Guard Your Mind!

An American Life!

Riley Miller's World View
Future President of USA
9-11's Deal
World Trade Center
Al Qaeda

Osama Bin Laden
Saddam Hussein
Terrorist Operations
Iraq and Iran War
Baghdad
ISIS Terrorist Group

Why, do we go to WW3?
The American Antichrist

How does American win?
Following The Antichrist To War

What is WWIII?
The Apocalypse of Armageddon

How is WW3 Fought?
Weapons of Mass Destruction of USA

Who Wins WW3?
America Wins

Why is it WW3?
The New World Order's Ending!

What does Christ do?
Rider on the White Horse

How WW3 Is Everyday?

Tomorrow
Everyone
Sundays
Everything
Everyday's
Each Day
All Days
New Days
Today
Living

WW3 Is Extinct!

Failure
Lost
Tries
Losses
Understanding
Damnation
Knowledge
Damned
Intelligent
Hell
Loss Days
Satan
Good Days
Hellishness
Peace

Life And Life's!

Pen
Hand
Sword
Side
Life
Deaths
Under
Armor
Pen
Side
Nail
Foot
Eyeballs
Contact Lenses
Forehead
Hat Brim
Head
Cowboy Hat

Death And Deals!

Sword
Sheath
Shot
Gun
Wound
Chest

Knife
Wastes

World War Three!

Expense
World Wars
Spending
Learning
Funding
Supportive
Lending
Participant
Sharing
Mutuality
Giving
Lending

(How Money Is Plan)

The USA'S Money!

Wealth of people in WW3
Poorest of those for WW3
Richest of loaners of WWIII
Paid highest of loot for WWIII
Surplus of money in WWIII
Lowest possible in WWIII
High earned dollar valued
Big expenses paid back to

No money earned for value
Giving money to World War

Money Meant Wars!

Richest Due to WW3
Least for WW3 In Support
Support through Loans to WW3
Highest Monetary Involved WW3
Most Support for WW3!
No Support from These People
Supported by Giving to Wars
No Show, No Dough in Wars
By Giving then Big Receiving

Big-Top From WW3's War!

Highest
Entertainment
Payments

Royalty
Payments
Dollars

Checks
Bill
Dollar

Big

Texas

USA

Pens

Signs

Signature

A Sealed Plan – WWIII'S USA!

Payments
Banks
Work
Spending
Cash
Accumulated Money
Big Earnings
Riches
Surplus
Money
Cash
Wealth
Banks
Fed
Office

The Lives Before War!!

Illuminati
Secret Plans
Hidden Agenda
Brotherhoods
Society
Groupings
Movements
Sealed Size
Measured
Republican
Democrat
Conservative
Predetermined
Ready
Sold

The Groups Movements To WW3

Secret
Public
Numerous
Heaven
American
Christian
Growing
Numbering
Larger

Books
Conspiracy
Theory
Mind
Clues
Sad

The Growing Movements To WW3!

Atomic
Nuclear
Biological
Racism
Anti-American
Selectivity
Foreign
Enemy
Holocaust
Bombs
Solders
USA Leads
One Man
One Country
One Enemy

WW3 – Plans To Takeover All

Selective
Characters
Holy Bible
Global

Movements
Strength
Time
Life
Human
Evil
Good
Will
Power
Enemy
Love
Strive
Hardest
Anger
Big
Sizable
Grows
Spreads
Catches-On
Returns
Every
All
Tripled
Size
Height
Weight
Pro
Con
Null
Force
Power

Enemy
Home
Family
Sacred
Large
Big
Giant
Grows
Forward
Omniscience
End
Talking
Thinking
Dumb
Smart
Mighty

When WW3 Begins, What's?

Communications
Talking
Speaking
All Over
Every Corner
Each Side
Fast
Slowest
Beginnings
Starts
First

New
Fear
Love
Purpose
Shock
Killing
Hatred
Ability
Happy
Smiles
Impacting
Television
Friend
Sides
Choices
Willing
Knowledge
Commentary
Destruction
Frontal
Measured
Sizing
Judgment
Party
Related
Relativity
Evolution
Choices
Easiness
Frown
A-Bomb

Holocaust
Ends
Armageddon
"Hitler-Esque Man
Madman Leading
Questionable Life

World War III – Spreading Over Already!

Soon
Afterwards
Deaths
Camps
Bases
Hidden Spots
Designated
Area
Designed
Walls
Assassins
Miller, Riley
Words
Picture
Internet
Social
Professional
Academic
Towns
Country
Democracy

Lives
Death
Talking
Roads
Bridges
Streets
Captured
Convict
Imprisoned
Life
Beings
Existing
Paths
Roads
Traveled
Peace
War
Already
Secret
Hidden
Unknown
Private
Rooms
House
Demonstrations
Christianity
Churched
Schedule
Events
Christians
Programs

Systems
Confinement
Education
Masses
Idealist
Fast
All
Limits
Story
Tales
Plots
Main
Big
Middle
Front
Lined
Proud
Business
Commerce
Gaining
Law
Order
NOA!
Song
Battle
Sing
Protect
Heard
Dear
Pro-Life
Guards

Cursed
Thrones
Crowned
Castles
Visionary
Product
Illuminated
Weeds
Sicken
Weaken

NOA Or NWO – WWIII "OK"!

NOA
Age Movement
Same
Firstly
Last
3 Letters
King Making
New World Order
"NWO'S King"
NOA
New Order of the Ages
Novus Ordo Seclorum
N.W.O.
Latin
Tree
Family
Times

Old Age
New Ages
New Orders
Ordered
World
New
"Make Me King"
"As We Move"
Towards a "NWO"
Story
Battle
Prepare
Treatment
Royalty
New Aged Order
Places
Directions
Movements
Rules
Succeeds
Provides
Wealth
Abundance
Necessities
War
Living
Ruling
Strong
Loud
Silent
Proud

Big
Content
Product
Source
Provision
Transparent
Motionless
Motioning
Crowds
Personifying
Strongest
King
New
Order
Every
One
Thing
Not
Is
Isn't
Worth
Value
Rightness
Noteworthy
Practiced
Valuable
Against
Wills
Protagonist
War
Legion

Faction
Spiritual
Leadership
Foundation
Physical
Emotional
Intellectuals
Mistakes
Errors
Wrongs
Brains
Brawn
Know
Young
Prides
Values
Oldest
Aged
Order
Sciences
Physicality
Directions
Medications
Bandages
Syringes
War's
Peaceful
Times

The Road Less Traveled On-

That Has Made All The Difference!

Know
Sense
Awareness
Crowds
Biggest
Lives
Supporting
Holding
Building-Up
Partings
Eventually
Diverging
Challenges
Out Measurable
Willpowers
Parting
Ways
Separated
Differenced
Wayward
Directionally
Found
Support
Travels
Ending
Stopping
Point
Separated
Differenced

Wayward
Directionally
Found
Support
Travels
Ending
Stopping
Point
Separating
Learnable
Took
Less
More
Roads

The Roads To WWIII!

Firstly
Chosen
Arranged
Presumably
Guessed
Calculate
Know
Hire
Concerned
Ability
Trajectory
Target
Miserable

Calculated
Misleading
Found
Traded
Disclosed
Numbered
Calculated
Measured
Christian
Unbelievable
Faithful
Righteous
Considered
Valueless
Hard
High
Climb
Discovery
Agreeableness
Valuable

The Hard Way – To WWIII?

Antisocial
Unbelieving
Weakest
Strongly
Kinds
Prophetic

Knights
Darkened
Founded
Different
Divisions
Directed
Roads
Whole
Intersections
Lighted
Chosen
Left
Right
Wrongful
Directly
Alone
Woods
Divided
Destination
Unknowing
Evaluated
Choice
Proud
Rewarded
Paths
Straight
Unconformity
Story
Tale
Endings
Nuclear

Atomic
Weapons
America
Divisions
Straight
Forwards
Divided
Resumed
Repeated
Proclaim
Resounded
Valued
Limitless
Holocaust's
Desecration
Tragedy
Found-Out
Dead
Silence

The WWIII Stage!

Tanks
Guns
Soldiers
Ammunition
Infantry
Slaughtering
Killing

Graves
Losing
Rest
Death
Burials
Topics
Strangers
Personalities
Lives
Dreamt
Condemned
Lifelessness
Trail
Human
Directed
Founded
Saved
Dead
Alive
Harden
Souls
Ditched
Found Again
Rediscovered
Remade
Resounded
Limitless
Find
Lived
Became
Questioned

Unknown
War
Friends
Foes

What Repeats History?
Is WW3 Relived Again?

New Order
New World Order
New Aged Order
Ordered
Repeated
Aged Thrice
Tripled War
One World
Two Sides
Divided
Humungous
Separated
Allied
Joined
Good Sided
Evil
Opponents
Homeliness
Joint
Twice
Friends

Divided
Deaths
Orders
Divine
Wicked
Twofold
One World
Another World
Both "New" Ordered
Worldviews
Heroes
Villains
Gone
Won
USA
Alive
Dead
Found
Strength
Deaths
Godspeed!
Government
New World Order
Antichrist's WWIII
End Times
Biblical American's WW3
Governing Bodies
Dead USA Party
USA
Endings
Deaths

All of It
Dead and Gone
The End Is Near
History of Wars
Third War of Worlds
World War Three
Under USA Law
Be an American
Try WW3 American
Jesus Christ In WWIII
God the Father In Ending
The Church In Apocalypse
World War of NWO
History of WWIII to WW3!
The Military Genius of USA's!
The WWIII
The End of Creation in WW3!
The End of USA!
War Times in A.C.'S USA
The Loss of All Lives
The Lasting Endings Of Itself –
WW3 Intellect Is In Secret Societies
American Plans From Old Retold War Lives
Remembering The History's Warred Figures
Costing The Price To Pay, To Lives Whom Lost
Comparing Presidential Books And War Books, Of
WWIII
Life And Death, To Wins Over WW3

To Try To Win! WW3!

USA
WW3
"A.C."
USA'S Antichrist One World
Sold to World Democracy
Bought By Final Offers
First One-World Government
Shadow Laws
One World Government
NOA
America's First Democracy
The Entire USA
All USA Followers of World
The New World Order
The Free World
Leader of Free World
Antichrist America
WWIII However, Is Dead at USA Ending?

My Lesson In World War III –
The New World Order, Government!

Force of Real Law
Public Forces of Legalities
Private Function From NWO'S WWIII
The Party of the First Democracy
The Whole Worldwide Followers
Every Citizen Is Counted Included
Public Offices Serve Citizens

Governing Officials Served N.W.O.'S WW3
Private Functions Relive WWII
The Government Is One-World-Order
The Followers Are From All Worlds
The Democracy Is Public Decisions
The A.C. Of One Man Is Represented
The Beast's Followers are False People
Heaven Fell Apart When A.C.'S WWIII Is
Democracy Is Alive In USA
Follower's Party Agrees With New USA Order
The USA's N.W.O. Hires One-World Government
WW3 Presidential Office
Hired Office of WWIII – Govern World Democracy
1-World Government/ NWO
Antichristian Life Head Towards Presidential
Endings

! "THE THIRD WORLD WAR!" XXXX

What Riley Does, He Wills into Power! X
What Words, Are Written That Wills, Wars Into
Power?

I Wrote, The Books Of the History In Loving And
Living Everything In Life, To Its Greatest Form –
"Books Of The Best Quality, Never Intelligence To
Fail, And From Good Teaching, Comes
Knowledge, Inyo Easy Books, Greatest, Biggest,
Boldest, Smartest, Books As The Easiest To Read,

Into The Library's History, From Houston, Texas,
In To Of The Tiptop's Of The World!!!"

<u>A Bible Topic in My Holy Bible –</u>

<u>Pride Promotes Strife</u>

James 4 – 6
In NKJV Holy Bible

James 4 – 1

"Where do wars and fights come
From among you?
Do, they not come from your
Desires for *pleasure*,
That war in your members?

4 – 2

You lust and do not have.
You murder and covet and cannot obtain.
You fight, and war.
Yet you do not have because you do not ask.

4 – 3

You ask and do not receive,
Because you ask amiss,
That you may spend it on your pleasures.

4 – 4

Adulterers and Adulteresses!
Do you not know that friendship
With the world, is enmity with God?

Whoever therefore wants to be a
Friend of the world makes himself
An enemy of God.

4 – 5

Or do you think that the Scripture
Says in vain, "The Spirit who
Dwells in us yearns jealously?"

4 – 6

But He gives more grace.
Therefore He says:

"God resists the proud,
But gives grace to the humble."

Titus 2 – 14

Who gave Himself for us,
That He might redeem us
From every lawless deed
And purify for Himself
His own special people,
Zealous for good works.

From-
The Epistle of James

Jesus Christ In Bible's Verses –
The Holy Bible
    The 'New King James' Version

A Book Solely By; "Riley Miller" – RPM!

Written in the Codex, Of The Book's Code – Ω!

Riley Miller
Read The Books From Myself
RPM